"With this superb book, Dr. Sharon D. Raynor has unlocked what she terms the "the transformative power involved in practicing veterans oral history for both the veteran and the interviewer." Raynor's book is a beautiful intersection of two key areas: first, it is an expert how-to guide to conducting individual and group veterans' histories; and, second, poignant meditations on the relationship of memory, trauma, and voice, as these have emerged in her own family's experiences. This is a pathbreaking addition that will enable veterans to speak through their own voices, gain self-understanding, and illuminate the complex worlds through which veterans have journeyed."

—Harlan Joel Gradin, PhD, Scholar Emeritus,
North Carolina Humanities

"To know Dr. Sharon D. Raynor is to witness her passion for veterans. We met when I had been awarded a grant from the North Carolina Humanities Council. Dr. Raynor was selected as a mentor to help me continue my documentary work with Vietnam veterans. I was soliciting and curating, for the first time, their personal photographs and remembrances. As a Vietnam-era veteran and documentarian, I felt it was my responsibility to help them "show what they couldn't say." Because Dr. Raynor was working on veterans' oral and recorded histories as well, she was invaluable. Her most important piece of advice about my work was to first create trust – and a dialog – with the men and women. Those heartfelt guidelines that comprise this book are a gift to anyone who wants to create that safe place for veterans of all ages who, deep inside, want to share their experiences. Thank you, Dr. Raynor. Job well done!"

—Martin Tucker; Vietnam-era Veteran; Photojournalist and Filmmaker;
Author, *Vietnam Photographs From North Carolina Veterans: The Memories
They Brought Home*

"Through her tremendous personal connection to our Veterans, Dr. Sharon D. Raynor has written an insightful must-read book that serves as a powerful blueprint, comprehensively outlining the process and techniques of orally capturing the history, personal stories, and encounters of America's heroes, our Veterans. I highly recommend this book and commend Dr. Raynor for her many contributions in support of our U.S. Armed Forces."

— Lieutenant Colonel Rob Freeman, U.S. Army

PRACTICING ORAL HISTORY WITH MILITARY AND WAR VETERANS

Practicing Oral History with Military and War Veterans focuses predominantly on conducting oral history with men and women of recent wars and military conflicts.

The book provides a structured methodology for building interest and trust among veterans to conduct interviews, design oral history projects, and archive and use these oral history interviews. It includes background on the evolution of veterans oral history, the nuts and bolts of interviewing, ethical guidelines, procedures, and the overall value of veterans oral history. The methodology emphasizes how memory evolves over the years – when a veteran becomes more distant from the events of war, the experiences become individualized and personalized for each veteran based on location, time, place, and purpose of their service. The book also aims to improve understanding of the personal, ethical, and psychological issues involved in listening compassionately to veterans' stories that may contain issues of trauma, gender, socioeconomics, race, dis/ability, and ethnicity.

Practicing Oral History with Military and War Veterans is an invitation to community scholars, students, oral historians, and families of veterans to actively participate in the oral history process and to embrace methodology that may help with designing and conducting oral history projects and interviewing war veterans.

Sharon D. Raynor currently serves as the Dean of the School of Humanities and Social Sciences (including the Military Science & Army ROTC Programs) and the Winnie Wood Endowed Professor of English and Digital Media at Elizabeth City State University. She uses her various platforms to share veterans' stories. Raynor is the executive producer for the documentary film, *In the Face of Adversity: The Service and Legacy of African American WWII Veterans* (2021 Longleaf Film Festival Official Selection) in support of the North Carolina African American Veterans Lineage Day Documentary Project and in collaboration with the NC Department of Military and Veterans Affairs, NC Museum of History, and NC

Humanities. She is also a co-producer of *The Silence of War*, a transmedia and short film documentary in collaboration with *The Imagination Project* at Wake Forest University's Documentary Film Program. Her website, "When Writing Goes to War: Stories from Black Veterans of North Carolina" (*www.whenwritinggoestowar. com*), highlights the culmination of her veterans oral history projects. Raynor is the co-editor of *Teaching Race in Perilous Times: Racial Discourse in the College Classroom* with SUNY Press. She has dedicated publications to veteran issues such as: "Breaking the Silence: The Unspoken Brotherhood of Vietnam Veterans," "The First Saddest Day of My Life: A Vietnam War Story," "The Double Consciousness and Disability Dilemma: Trauma and the African American Veteran," "African American Masculinity Performance in the Diaries of Vietnam Soldiers," "The Tell-Tale-Listener: Gendered Representations in Oral History [with Vietnam Veterans]," "Welcome Home, Brother," " 'Sing a Song Heroic': Paul Laurence Dunbar's Mythic and Poetic Tribute to Black Soldiers," and "Something He Couldn't Write About: Telling My Daddy's Story of Vietnam." Other diverse scholarly publications are in the areas of African American literary studies and narrative and trauma theory appear in *The Oral History Review*, *History Now* (Gilder-Lehrman Institute of American History), *Australian Feminist Review* and *The Yancy Years 1994–2008: The Age of Infrastructure, Technology & Restoration*, and *27 Views of Charlotte: The Queen City in Prose and Poetry*.

She previously worked at East Carolina University, Johnson C. Smith University, Wake Forest University, and the Center for Documentary Studies at Duke University. Raynor has been a faculty fellow for the Gilder-Lehrman Institute of American History, Center for the Study of Race, Ethnicity and Gender in the Social Sciences at Duke University, Clark-Yudkin Research Fellowship for United States Air Force Academy, *Humanities Writ Large* Faculty Fellowship at Duke University and Center for Documentary Studies and the Alphonse Fletcher, Jr., Fellowship at the W.E. B. DuBois Institute for African and African American Research at Harvard University, and the Faculty Resource Network Fellowship at New York University. She has participated in international faculty study abroad programs with the UNCF/Mellon Faculty Seminar Program in Salvador, Brazil and Cape Town, South Africa; The Salzburg Seminar in Salzburg, Austria; and the Council on International Educational Exchange in Dakar, Senegal and Cape Verde, West Africa. Raynor is a North Carolina native with degrees in English and Multicultural Literature (BA 1994, MA 1996) from East Carolina University and a PhD in Literature and Criticism (2003) from Indiana University of PA. She is the 2020 recipient of the Old North State Award from the North Carolina Governor's Office for her continuous work in the fields of education and veterans advocacy in the state of North Carolina.

Practicing Oral History

Series editor
Nancy MacKay

Museums, historical societies, libraries, classrooms, cultural centers, refugee organizations, elder care centers, and neighborhood groups are among the organizations that use oral history both to document their own communities and to foster social change. The *Practicing Oral History* series addresses the needs of these professionals with concise, instructive books about applying oral history best practices within the context of their professional goals.

Titles fall into one of three areas of applied oral history. The first format addresses a specific stage or skill within the oral history process. The second addresses the needs of professional communities who use oral history in their field. The third approach addresses the way oral history can be used to make an impact. Each title provides practical tools, ethical guidelines and best practices for conducting, preserving, and using oral histories within the framework of acknowledged standards and best practices.

Readers across a wide array of disciplines will find the books useful, including education, public history, local history, family history, communication and media, cultural studies, gerontology, documentary studies, museum & heritage studies, and migration studies.

Recent titles in the series

Creating Verbatim Theatre from Oral Histories
Clare Summerskill

Practicing Oral History with Military and War Veterans
Sharon D. Raynor

For more information, or to place orders visit Routledge, Practicing Oral History, www.routledge.com/Practicing-Oral-History/book-series/POHLCP

PRACTICING ORAL HISTORY WITH MILITARY AND WAR VETERANS

Sharon D. Raynor

NEW YORK AND LONDON

Designed cover image: Sharon D. Raynor

First published 2023
by Routledge
605 Third Avenue, New York, NY 10158

and by Routledge
4 Park Square, Milton Park, Abingdon, Oxon, OX14 4RN

Routledge is an imprint of the Taylor & Francis Group, an informa business

© 2023 Taylor & Francis

Library of Congress Cataloging-in-Publication Data
Names: Raynor, Sharon D., author.
Title: Practicing oral history with military and war veterans /
    Sharon D. Raynor.
Description: New York, NY : Routledge, 2023. | Series: Practicing oral
    history | Includes bibliographical references and index.
Identifiers: LCCN 2022032730 (print) | LCCN 2022032731 (ebook) |
    ISBN 9781629583501 (hardback) | ISBN 9781032248332 (paperback) |
    ISBN 9781003280323 (ebook)
Subjects: LCSH: Oral history. | United States—Armed Forces. |
    Veterans—United States—Interviews.
Classification: LCC D16.14 .R39 2023 (print) | LCC D16.14 (ebook) |
    DDC 907.2—dc23/eng/20220907
LC record available at https://lccn.loc.gov/2022032730
LC ebook record available at https://lccn.loc.gov/2022032731

ISBN: 978-1-62958-350-1 (hbk)
ISBN: 978-1-032-24833-2 (pbk)
ISBN: 978-1-003-28032-3 (ebk)

DOI: 10.4324/9781003280323

Typeset in Bembo
by Apex CoVantage, LLC

This book is dedicated to my Father and Vietnam Veteran, Louis Jerry Raynor, better known as "Smiley," who trusted me with his story and continuing his legacy of service to others; to my Mother, Katie Mae Raynor, who always nurtured my curiosity and creativity; and to "my guys," those Vietnam Veterans who started this journey with me, holding my hand along the way and blessing the telling of their stories: Robert Jones, Jr., Ronnie Stokes, Charles Helbig, John Barnes, Robert Jones, Tex Howard, and Ralph Shaw.

CONTENTS

FOREWORD

With photos and videos of war zones flashing across our screens relentlessly, it is nearly impossible to avoid the grim realities of war. So we turn off the screen or gloss over the image to avoid thinking about it and get on with our lives. That is easy for those of us who have never witnessed war firsthand, never had to watch, for example, "a squad leader at age 21, witnessing the deaths of younger squad members, the responsibility of having another's life in one's hands" (Chapter 15, p. 128). But for veterans of wars or armed conflicts, it is a different story. Veterans may carry memories for a long time, easily triggered by war photos, random conversations, sound of a siren, or other daily events. Time lightens these memories for most, but they never completely go away. In order to cope and to fit into civilian society, some veterans meet the world with a wall of silence, to protect themselves and their loved ones. Every veteran's story is unique and multifaceted. It is an effort to understand a veteran's silence, her father's, that led Sharon D. Raynor to her life work and to the writing of this book.

Sharon writes, "my work with Vietnam veterans was perhaps predestined. The last American troops withdrew from Vietnam on March 29, 1973; I was born the very next day. . . . As the daughter of a Vietnam veteran, I was constantly seeking answers to questions about the war and the profound silence that engulfed my family. . . . I lived with my father's silence about the war for several decades. As a child, I often wondered what happened to him during that war that could create such a profound and deafening silence" (Chapter 3, p. 17). In four sections, Sharon weaves the threads of her personal story, her professional work with veterans, and an instruction manual into a book that is practical, informative, and deeply personal.

In Section I, Sharon tells her own story as the daughter of a Vietnam Veteran growing up in a large and close-knit family, the confusing silences about certain topics, and the decades it took her to understand that her father's behavior was rooted in love and a desire to protect his family from experiences they could never comprehend. Sharon grew up, attended college and attracted to the concept of narrative, and became a professor of literature. Her professional work attracted the attention of veterans' organizations, and she began interviewing veterans. As word spread, she found herself interviewing war veterans who had had experiences much like her father's. Eventually, Sharon's professional connection to war veterans brought father and daughter closer.

Sharon's personal story sets the stage for the following sections standard in *Practicing Oral History* titles – best practices, ethics, a step-by-step guide to designing and conducting an oral history project, considerations of archiving, and the importance of oral histories finding their intended audience.

Section II, Issues Common in Veterans Oral History, considers the human side of veterans oral history. It begins with a chapter on ethical guidelines in doing oral history based on the best practices of the Oral History Association (US) and the Veterans History Project, concluding with an important reminder that oral historians are usually not psychologists, lawyers, and correctional officers, and there are times when an expert must be consulted. Topics include ways of building trust, making space for silence, understanding trauma, and using patience to cultivate relationships with the veteran. Sharon writes,

> I spent a tremendous amount of time with my core group of veterans by visiting their homes and seeing them in various settings. Others who have worked with me on projects have also done the same, like going fishing, spending time going through old photographs, visiting their farms or joining them with their hobbies. The trust you take the time to develop when getting to know the veteran will allow you to accomplish the goals and objectives of your oral history project.
>
> *(Chapter 6, p. 54)*

From this thoughtful introduction to veterans oral history, Sharon continues in Sections III and IV to present the nuts and bolts of planning, conducting, and archiving veterans' oral histories. She begins Chapter 8, Project Planning and Preparation, by calling for an important decision to be made at the beginning of any oral history project: who is the intended audience for the interviews? Veterans' oral histories are commonly done as family documentation, as community history, or as research documents to be available in libraries and archives. The answer to this question is essential to the project planning and everything thereafter because each scenario requires a different approach to project design, the final home for the interview, and even the questions asked in the interview. Don't worry. Sharon guides the reader through the planning steps for each scenario. She encourages readers to involve veterans in the project, not only as interviewees but also as subject specialists, transcribers, researchers, or interviewers, and offers important tips about recording equipment, interviewing techniques, and doing remote interviews.

And there is more: the book is filled with best practices, insights from Sharon's own work and from other veterans oral history projects, a section on memory and trauma, a section on distance interviewing, and practical advice on recording equipment in different situations, including an interesting section on why Sharon has switched from audio to video recording interviews.

Midway through the writing of this book, Sharon's father passed away from a cancer induced by his exposure to Agent Orange in Vietnam so many years ago. Sharon needed to step back from writing for a while, to spend time with family, and to allow her grief to find its center. She returned to this book with a deeper, more empathetic approach to the topic, something that can only be achieved through personal experience. As she acknowledges in Chapter 1, "the best books are lived before they are written" (Chapter 1, p. 3). That describes the book you hold in your hands.

I am so very pleased to present this as the eleventh title in the *Practicing Oral History* series.

Nancy MacKay
Berkeley, California
June 2022

PREFACE

As the daughter of a Vietnam Veteran and a practitioner of veterans oral history, I am writing this book to invite community scholars, students, oral historians, and families of veterans to actively participate in the oral history process with war veterans and to embrace this methodology that may help with designing and conducting oral history projects, and to interviewing war veterans. While this book may prove helpful when conducting oral history with war veterans of all generations, it focuses predominantly on conducting oral history with men and women of recent wars and military conflicts. The methodology in this book emphasizes how memory evolves over the years when a veteran becomes more distant from the events of war and the experiences becomes individualized and personalized for each veteran based on location, time, place, and purpose of his service. When a veteran rethinks his experiences out of the military environment, he begins to attach meaning and give voice to those events.

This book is to provide a structured methodology for building interest and trust among veterans to conduct interviews, design oral history projects, and archive and use these oral history interviews. This book provides background on the evolution of veterans oral history, the nuts and bolts of interviewing, ethical guidelines, procedures, and the overall value of veterans oral history. This book is to also help understand the personal, ethical, and psychological issues in compassionately listening to veterans' stories that may involve issues of trauma, gender, socioeconomics, race, dis/ability, and ethnicity.

This methodology will encourage readers and practitioners to move beyond the mere collection of stories and toward acknowledging and recognizing veterans oral history as a therapeutic healing process that often creates community support. I hope to motivate readers to seek out those stories that you long to hear from veterans in your families and communities. I hope that you will invite a veteran, or several, to sit with you and talk about their wartime experiences.

I hope this methodology will guide and encourage you in the veterans oral history process. The book is a practical guide for those specifically interested in interviewing war veterans, whether for a private family history or for a more formal, structured oral history project.

I have been in higher education for nearly twenty-five years and as I have aged, my students have only gotten younger or so it seems. With their youth also came the differences in our generations, so I discovered over the years that how they learn and what they are interested in knowing changes rapidly. I would often allow students to offer suggestions about class readings, films, and assignments. We built our classroom community based on their willingness to participate and learn. With this book and methodology, there will be sections that illustrate how younger generations can engage with veterans oral history in ways that may make sense only to them. After discussions with my colleagues and students, I wanted to make sure that certain subject matter was also included in the book.

Scope of the Book

The scope of this book encompasses all those military personnel in various branches who served in both combat and noncombat roles, mostly US military and war veterans with living memories, inclusive of men, women, various races and ethnic identities, multiple wars, and conflicts. Since the scope of the book covers a methodology for practicing oral history with military and war veterans, I want to provide a brief history of America's participation in wars and conflicts since World War II (WWII), which now are the oldest living veterans. Reportedly, the last World War I (WWI) veterans passed away in 2011.

For this book, I define American participation by the "boots on the grounds" concept in which US troops had an active presence in these conflicts and/or wars. Without going into detail as whether each was an actual war or a conflict or the exact reasons, which are often debatable for America's participation, this synopsis will help oral historians and documentarians better understand how soldiers and veterans could serve in multiple conflicts/wars and have several deployments during their military service. It is also important to note that the United States still has active-duty military personnel in various regions around the world. It is often through oral history when those who participated and fought in these wars and conflicts actually share their personal beliefs about why the United States was involved. Whether they agreed with the reasoning or not, they all answered their call to serve.

Figure 1 highlights the wars and conflicts that veterans you interview may have been involved in and chose to talk about during their interviews.

Beyond just the Army, Navy, Air Force, Marines, and Coast Guard military service (including all reserve units), this methodology will expand the military branches to include participants in veterans oral history: Air Force Nurse Corps, Army Air Forces/Corps, Army Nurse Corps, Cadet Nurse Corps, Merchant Marine, Navy Nurse Corps, SPAR (Women's Coast Guard Reserve), Women's

Years	War/Conflict	Involvement
1939-1945	World War II	United States joined forces with Great Britain's Frances and Russia to fight against Axis Power (Germany, Italy and Japan
1950-1953	Korean War	United States fought with South Korea as a part of the United Nations against North Korea and Communist China
1961	Bay of Pigs	United States invaded Cuba during the Bay of Pigs
1960-1971	Vietnam War	United States and South Vietnam joined forces against North Vietnam
1983	Grenada	United States invaded the Caribbean island of Grenada
1989	Operation Just Cause	United States Invaded Panama
1990-1991	Persian Gulf War (This is also known as the First Gulf War, The Invasion of Kuwait, Operation Desert Shield and Operation Desert Storm)	United States and Coalition Forces fought against Iraq.
1995-1996	Intervention in Bosnia and Herzegovina	United States, as a part of NATO acted as peacekeepers in the former Yugoslavia.
2001-2021	Invasion of Afghanistan (2001 marked the beginning of Operation Enduring Freedom (OEF), which was the official name of the Global War on Terror)	United States along with Coalition Forces fought against the Taliban regime in Afghanistan
2003-2011	Invasion of Iraq	United States once again along with Coalition Forces fought against Iraq
2004-present	War in Northwest Pakistan	United States fought against Pakistan, mostly drone attacks
2007-present	Somalia and Northeastern Kenya	United States and Coalition forces fought against the militants in Somalia and Northeastern Kenya
2009-2016	Operation Ocean Shield -Indian Ocean	United States fought with NATO against Somali pirates
2011	Libya	The United States and NATO allies fought against Libya
2011-2017	Uganda	The United States and allies fought against the Lord's Resistance Army
2014-2017	Iraq	The United States and Coalition forces led an intervention in Iraq against the Islamic State of Iraq and Syria
2014-present	Syria	The United States and Coalition forces led an intervention in Syria against al-Qaeda, ISIS and Syria
2015-present	Yemeni Civil War	United States joined with the Saudi-led coalition to fight against rebels in Yemen
2015-present	Libya	United States and Libya led an intervention in Libya against ISIS.

FIGURE 1   *American Involvement in Wars From Colonial Times to the Present Wars From 1675 to the Present Day*[1]

Army Auxiliary Corps (WAAC), Women's Army Corps (WAC), Women Airforce Service Pilots (WASP), Navy Women's Reserve (WAVES), and Women Marines.

Throughout the book, I use the term "military veterans" when I refer to military personnel who did not engage in combat in any situation and "war veterans" when I refer to those who actively participated in either an armed conflict and/or a designated war. I use the term "war" to include armed conflicts, even though there are historical distinctions between the two. Some veterans have served in both armed conflicts and war zones. My father always talked about the importance of support personnel during the war. Those who served in the "rear" and not on the "frontlines" were essential to operations and survival. The experiences and stories are often intertwined when talking about war. The methodology will highlight the significance of the veterans oral history interview by focusing on the purpose for the documentation and oral history project. While practicing oral history with combat war veterans may require a specific understanding of trauma, silence, and memory, an oral history interview with a military noncombat veteran may provide significant information and perspective about a specific time and place that help tell the entire story. Military veterans who may not necessarily have a "combat story" – deserve to have their voice heard in the same way as their colleagues in combat do. In an attempt to include those experiences and stories that are not often heard (the underlying premise of oral history), I will discuss ways to be inclusive – in project design, in the interview itself, and in forms of access to the interview, remembering that no one is exempt from potential trauma.

Clearly, inclusivity with regard to race and gender is essential when gathering all sides of a story. For the sake of clarity, I will use the gender pronoun "he" when referring to both male and female soldiers as a group, though my decision is grounded in a desire for readability and is not intended to lessen the role of women in the military and in combat in any way. When I refer specifically to the experiences and stories of women in the military, I use the feminine pronouns. Throughout the book, the voices, experiences, and stories of women in the military, who served in various capacities, will be present and in some way, offering their perspective on issues that are specifically female. These issues might include: reasons why they served, sexual harassment and misconduct in the military, motherhood, hygiene issues (such as availability of products), changing rules regarding women's hairstyles, dress/clothing, stereotypes and prejudices, war injuries and post-traumatic stress disorder (PTSD) as it is experienced by women, combat, promotions in service, and issues with authority/facing issues when they are a high-ranking official.

Witnessing my father's health challenges and his death made me further realize how important it is to focus a bit on how a veteran's disabilities and/or injuries can affect the interview and what we as oral historians, storytellers, and family members should be aware of when planning to interview a veteran. It becomes very important for the interviewer to have an understanding of the VA medical system, VA services and resources, and its disability rating system in case it is mentioned during the interview – preparation to help with follow-up questions or a basic understanding would allow for a more natural flow of the interview and narrative process.

Throughout the book, I will refer to the veterans projects that I have been involved with over the last twenty or so years along with other examples of existing veterans oral history projects. This work for me, like many other everyday people, along with oral historians and documentarians, is very personal. Oral history, in general, but especially veterans oral history has a unique way of changing lives. In every aspect, the subject is more than the just the oral history project because the veterans could require additional care and attention throughout the process.

Note

1   American Involvement in Wars from Colonial Times to the Present Wars from 1675 to the Present Day. *ThoughtCo.* www.thoughtco.com/american-involvement-wars-colonial-times-present-4059761. Accessed November 7, 2021.

ACKNOWLEDGMENTS

"Greater love hath no man than this, that a man lay down his life for his friends."
—John 15:13 KJV

This book has definitely been in production for far too long, and so this process reminds me of a song lyric: "every story has its scars." Those words seem quite appropriate for such a time as this. Practicing military and veterans oral history can involve a shared sense of belonging, community, trauma, recovery, and healing. I am thankful for all the service men and women for their sacrifices and for every story that was shared with me. I hope it helped, if just a little, heal those scars and wounds of war that affect so many soldiers, veterans, families, and communities. To the Vietnam Veterans and their families who began this work with me: Louis J. Raynor, Robert Jones, Jr., Tex Howard, Charles Helbig, Ralph Shaw, John Barnes, Ronnie Stokes, and Robert Jones, I salute you, because I know that the stories I heard, your stories, have indeed helped heal some of my own scars.

"A friend loveth at all times, and a brother is born for adversity."
Proverbsr17:17 KJV

So many people were instrumental in this process because, at times, I needed all the encouragement and motivation to continue. The death of my dad, Louis J. Raynor, devastated not only my life but also my writing process. I no longer saw the importance of this book project. My grief was relentless, and my energy to move forward was fleeting. Besides, my work with documenting the wartime experiences of veterans started because of my dad. Since he was no longer here, I continued to ask myself: what was the point, his story ended much too soon, as so many other veterans, by losing his battle with cancer (a service-connected cancer, by the way), so what was left to say or do?

After years of actually practicing military and veterans oral history in various ways, I was fortunate to find an editor who thought the methodology of this specific scholarship was worthy of a book. My editor, Nancy MacKay, immediately recognized my hesitation to continue to write while also acknowledging my loss and grief. Her compassion afforded me the time needed to process my loss. The many conversations with Nancy helped me once again recognize the value and significance of my work. She read many drafts, providing suggestions and edits that proved to be a game changer. Thank you, Nancy, for being that guiding light and quiet motivational whisper that pushed me to complete this book.

Thank you to my mother, Katie, for the encouragement and for reminding me of who I am, why I started this work, and the need to complete it even in the face of loss, and to my late father for allowing me to become his legacy and letting his memory live on through storytelling. Thank you, to my siblings, family, and friends: Cassandra, Patrick, Jerry, Amanda, Tosha, Amaris, Donald, Edna, Vanessa, Shironda, Markiest Waller, and Janelle Martin for always supporting my work and constantly reminding me to take breaks, to enjoy naps, and to laugh often. To my youngest sister, Marquitta, and friend, Christopher Chesnutt, thanks for your endearing support and making sure that the digital and visual components of my work were always perfect. To my Bermudian friend, Nicole Simons, thank you for sharing your culture, courage, and strength. You are earth + wind + fire. To my Australian friend, Annette Houlihan, thank you for simply being my friend throughout this writing journey. May your soul find peace. To my dear friend, Raynard K. Townsel, the one who knows me best of all, thank you for sharing your Universe: wisdom, time, space, and energy. For you, I am grateful . . . next lifetime, my friend, next lifetime.

To my amazing mentors, thank you, Dr. Harlan Gradin, for being with the North Carolina Humanities at the beginning of the work in 1999 and for being steadfast and supportive ever since by reading and revising manuscript pages and calling to talk about the actual "writing" of the book. You are my soul's inspiration in this story community. Thank you, Dr. Dorothy Cowser Yancy, Dr. Marilyn Sutton-Haywood, and Mr. Gerald Hector, for keeping me inspired as a writer and informed as a scholar while navigating higher education. Thank you, Martin Tucker, for continuing to practice military and veterans oral history with me, reading pages of my manuscript and also reminding me of the importance of our work. Thank you to the many counselors and practitioners at the Greenville Veterans Outreach Center and the Raleigh Veterans Outreach Center, who supported my work and to the many service men and women who attended community events, shared their experiences, and participated in interview sessions.

Thank you to my colleagues and students at East Carolina University, especially Dr. Chip Sullivan and Dr. Jim Kirkland, where my oral history work first blossomed and at Johnson C. Smith University where my work was given enough light to grow. Thank you to my Elizabeth City State University colleagues who worked with me on military and veterans documentary (arts) projects, shared their ideas, inspired my work, and gave life to the many collected stories: Clarence Goss, Kelly Ford, Joyce Shaw, Jeff Whelan, Dr. Chyna Crawford, MSG Keith Nile (retired), LTC Robert Freeman, Dr. Adam McKee, and Dr. Jeffrey Rousch and to the many graphic design, digital media, and history students who participated in my military and veterans oral history projects over the years. A special thanks to the cadets of the ECSU US Army SROTC (Senior Reserve Officer Training Corp) Cadre – Viking Battalion – for their participation and inspiration during these projects. Thank you, to my Wake Forest University colleagues in the Documentary Film program, Sandy Dickson, Cara Pilson and Cindy Hill for embracing my work as a part of *The Imagination Project* and transforming the veterans' stories into visual art. Thank you to my *Humanities Writ Large* colleagues and friends, Dr. Jason Cohen and Dr. Tess Chakkalakal, who ran around Duke University's campus with me as we all explored our paths and expanded our research. The many long days and late nights, conversations over coffee, and ongoing collaborations are invaluable to me as a scholar.

I
Introduction

1

MY STORY

"For in death there is no remembrance of thee:
in the grave who shall give thee thanks?"
Psalms 6:5

My Story

I once read two things that inspired me as I was trying to complete this book. First, "I've learned that the best books are lived before they are written. True transformation takes place when information collides with revelation. Until I lived the chapters, they couldn't come together correctly. After much time and many tears, I know in my heart that now is the time." Second and by far the most powerful, was, "cancer lies. At worst, it kills. At the very least, it robs you of your joy" (Gray 167). Let me explain.

Writing and completing this book have been both personal and difficult for me because just a few years ago, my father, Louis Jerry Raynor, who served with the Third Squad/Fifth Cavalry, Nineth Infantry Division, Black Knights in the US Army, was diagnosed with multiple myeloma, a blood cancer that was service-connected to his exposure to Agent Orange while serving in Vietnam from 1967 to 1968. This, along with several other service-connected disabilities and illnesses and injuries, further complicated his life. While witnessing his health slowly decline and how the various chemotherapy treatments changed his life, most days I realized that he did not feel much like talking or sharing. He had become silent about his wartime experiences, once again. I was fortunate enough to have documented many of his experiences before this diagnosis. On December 28, 2018, my father passed away.

Cancer not only lied but also killed. Worse and far more devastating is the fact that cancer robbed me of my joy. So, I stopped writing. It was too painful. This book probably should have been finished a few years ago, but my work with

DOI: 10.4324/9781003280323-2

veterans has always paralleled my father's life. When he was first diagnosed, five years prior to his death, my entire life changed. I wanted to help take care of him and to be at the Veterans Administration (VA) hospital with him and my mother for appointments, treatments, and aftercare, so my professional work with veterans slowed down a bit. I was teaching and writing less. The subject matter made writing this book even more complicated. Quite a bit was written, edited, and revised while sitting in my father's hospital room. Along with my mother and other siblings, we would sit vigilantly as doctors, nurses, specialists, and medical students came and went. They would be busy checking his vitals, administering tests, and poking and probing, taking his blood in ongoing speculative fashion since there was no cure for blood cancer. There were even times when the cancer was undetectable in my father's blood, but that, of course, was always temporary, based on how his body responded to whichever chemotherapy that he was receiving at the time. Over the years, the care at the VA hospital had slightly improved. My father was always in the cancer unit with a private room with a shared bathroom, where the nurses recognized him as a regular patient. The nurses' familiarity with him and the fact that we were always present at the hospital advocating for him which often led to better care.

Spending so much time at the VA hospital, I couldn't help but notice all the other veterans who had no family members or loved ones nearby; they were just alone. It broke my heart. On more than a few occasions, my family and I would assist a veteran to find an appointment room or just to have a conversation. These small gestures can lift a veteran's spirits, if only momentarily. During my father's stays at the hospital, he would often run into other veterans he knew from his readjustment counseling groups at the Raleigh Veterans Outreach Center or even from our oral history projects. Regardless of their physical conditions, their recognition of each other was always immediate; the stories would start to flow, and their laughter and affection for each other were infectious.

Sometimes, I felt like I was writing against time; each setback or hospital visit seemed to interrupt my ability to move forward through this book project. It was quite difficult to explain my feelings to friends and colleagues who had not experienced this kind of life with a veteran. My father's willingness to still share stories and experiences with me at this stage of his life seemed remarkable, given his health conditions. That is the beauty of storytelling. Once the process starts, it will continue organically, on its own, without much effort at all. I had to accept that my father had come to terms with his own death, when he called me late one night and told me to make sure that his medical records were up to date with this diagnosis of multiple myeloma. Even though I did not want to have this conversation with him, he told me that it was important because this diagnosis had a terminal prognosis and he wanted to ensure my mother would receive the automatic military death benefit. He was already making preparations so my mother would be properly taken care of when he was gone.

As my father's health gradually changed and declined, I knew that things would never be the same again. After being at the VA hospital with a bout of pneumonia after Thanksgiving, we were told that there were no more available chemo options to treat his blood cancer. We had exhausted all possibilities during the five-year period, and I knew that my father was growing more and more tired of the weekly trips to the hospital for treatments, the ongoing regimen at home, and sometimes extended hospital stays. He had already grown silent. The palliative care team at the hospital, who visited us three days in a row, was very honest with us to make sure we understood that my father did not have much time left and there was nothing more, medically, that they could do. They discussed hospice care and how we could best make him comfortable at home and that we should take this time to be with him. My father was so brave hearing this news. He told us that he did not want to die at the VA hospital. He signed his "do not resuscitate orders" prior to leaving the hospital. He came home on hospice care on December 5. He was able to tell us exactly what he wanted, so we honored his wishes. Twenty-eight days later when he took his last breath a little before 4 AM, he was surrounded by his wife (my mother) of nearly fifty years of marriage and all of his children, just as he desired.

During these difficult first months of grief, I was constantly being pulled back to the work through a series of extraordinary circumstances, conversations, and people. I had a reputation for documenting the stories of veterans in North Carolina, so the phone began to ring and emails started pouring in requesting my help with projects. One of the projects that really helped pull me back to this work was my participation in the North Carolina African American Veterans Lineage Day (NCAAVLD) that was created and sponsored by the North Carolina Department of Military and Veterans Affairs and North Carolina Department of Military and Veterans Affairs (NCDMVA), the North Carolina Museum of History, and the North Carolina State Archive. This day was designed to honor, celebrate, and document the experiences of the African American veterans in North Carolina. Within just a few weeks, I was tasked to assemble a team of filmmakers, oral historians, and documentarians who could record the interviews, photograph the veterans and the activities, and then produce a documentary film that would showcase the events of that day. It was such an honor to be able to spend time with World War II veterans as they shared their life experiences with us. I worked with a team of creative colleagues and students from Elizabeth City State University to prepare these oral history interviews, document the events of the program, and produce a documentary film. As the North Carolina African American Veterans Lineage Day project continued, so has my work with honoring these men and women through oral history. During this particular project, we recognized World War II veterans from Montsford Point Marines, B1 Navy Band, Triple Nickle, the Fifth Calvary (original Calvary of the Buffalo Soldiers), 6888th Central Postal Directory Battalion, First Regiment N.C.C. Volunteers, Women's Army Auxiliary Corps, and Air Force Global Navigators. At the time of the project, the oldest of these veteran participants was ninety-nine years old, and she was still willing to share her stories and experiences.

This project is an example of how oral history projects with military and war veterans often evolve organically in order to capture a moment in time, to preserve historical memories as we are made aware of them, and to try to do this in the most ethical way possible often in a limited amount of time. These stories are often told first in a causal setting to someone who the veteran knows well. Once told the first time, the story or the story of the storyteller is often passed on by word of mouth to someone who may perhaps be interested in doing something more with these types of stories.

In a way, it was a full circle moment for me because when I was originally started an oral history project with Vietnam Veterans and they refused to work with me, it was a World War II veteran who convinced them to participate so future generations would know their story as well. He shared that he wished someone wanted to hear his story before he passed away because many of the battle buddies were gone. Once he spoke, the Vietnam Veterans were more willing to work with me. As much as I tried to stay away from working with veterans so soon after the loss of my dad, I could not avoid it. While at the NC Museum during this NCAAVLD program, I saw an exhibit curated by colleague, Martin Tucker, who I had not seen in almost fifteen years. His "A Thousand Words: Photographs by Vietnam Veterans" exhibit was on display. It quickly reminded me of the power of these images from Vietnam along with the introduction that I wrote for his project display. Martin and I had the opportunity to reconnect, and I invited him to my university to talk with students about his life and work as a veteran and photojournalist. His words connected to our students, and they were very interested in not only the stories of these veterans but also the photographs that they shared. He advised me to keep writing, documenting, and producing this work because the stories of Vietnam Veterans may no longer be told. He not only assured me that there was still an audience who needed to hear these stories, but it was also important that we teach others how to collect these stories to preserve them for future generations. These are the types of things I plan to discuss throughout the book.

The other veterans from my core group of the "Breaking the Silence" project encouraged me to stick with the work because it made such a difference in their lives. And then there was my mother who wanted the work to continue as a part of my father's legacy and the fact that he enjoyed the moments when he was with this brotherhood of Vietnam Veterans and how they took care of each other. My book editor, Nancy MacKay, was also instrumental in reminding me of just how much writing I had already completed before my dad got really sick and passed away. She helped me put the work back into perspective. Our veterans are dying at an astonishing rate, especially Vietnam Veterans, so I must continue to work to try to share as many of their stories as possible. Intellectually, I knew this, but emotionally I was not sure that I was ready for the journey to continue. My father left so much of himself in Vietnam and the pieces that he brought home, he eventually shared with his family, and I decided that I needed to definitely honor him and his service. After many months of not writing or focusing on this book project, I spent a lot of time in dark places crying with my computer or notepad scribbling down thoughts and ideas that could get me to the finish line. Some sections in the book are more personal than other sections, which is very intentional because sometimes these veterans stories can have an intimate nature, like those moments in my work that involved my father.

As my book nears completion and during Father's Day weekend in June 2022, my family and I traveled to Washington, DC to participate in the *InMemory* Ceremony sponsored and hosted by the Vietnam Veterans Memorial Fund (VVMF) to honor approximately 513 veterans who fought in Vietnam and later died after their return home due to Agent Orange and other service-related illnesses. My father was named to the 2022 *InMemory* Honor Roll. Although his name is not on The Wall, a plaque on the grounds of the Vietnam Veterans Memorial Site dedicated to these veterans reads, "In Memory of the men and women who served in the Vietnam War and later died as a result of their service. We honor and remember their sacrifices." Since the conception of *InMemory*, more than 5,000 veterans have been added to the honor roll.[1] My father, along with so many others, was finally honored for their service and sacrifice. During the ceremony, family members openly mourned the loss of their soldier but also honored their sacrifice with personal stories and memories.

Since I have spent over two decades entrenched in these stories, I wanted that sentiment to be a significant part of the methodology when practicing oral history with military and war veterans. This book is my contribution to the field of oral history and how to best practice this with military and war veterans.

Note

1   *InMemory* Program. www.vvmf.org/In-Memory-Program/

Bibliography

Gray, John. *I am Number 8: Overlooked and Undervalued, But Not Forgotten by God.* New York: Faith Works, 2017.

2

OVERVIEW AND EVOLUTION OF MILITARY AND VETERANS ORAL HISTORY

In 1983, it was noted that oral history was historically defined as "information that comes from interviewing persons who were present at events at issue" (Bennett 12). The Oral History Association defines it as "a field of study and a method of gathering, preserving and interpreting the voices and memories of people, communities, and participants in past events. Oral history is both the oldest type of historical inquiry, predating the written word, and one of the most modern, initiated with tape recorders in the 1940s and now using 21st-century digital technologies." Veterans oral history evolved into more than a collection of archival documents that provide information or as a gathering of a body of historical information in oral form usually on tape. "Because the scholarly community is usually involved in both the production and use of oral history, the *Oral History Association* recognizes an opportunity and an obligation on the part of all concerned to make this type of historical source as authentic and as useful as possible" (Fry 162). With the growing interdisciplinarity of oral history, other terminology exists, such as life histories, life stories, life documents, personal documents, life narratives, and auto/biographies.

In the late 1940s, Allan Nevins laid the foundation for the field we know today. He wanted the Columbia University Oral History Research Program to legitimize the methodology within the academy by grounding oral history interviews in extensive preparation. This includes recording interviews, preserving and cataloging them in an institutional or academic repository, and making them available to researchers. Both interviewer and interviewee should sign a legal release form which complies with laws of the land. At that time, the final product of the oral history interview was the transcript rather than the recording. Because the transcript could be used for research purposes, similar to other archival materials, it could be cataloged and indexed (Kuhn 97). Paul Thompson in *The Voice of the Past: Oral History* reminds us that oral history (which I would also include in veterans oral history), depends on the nature in which it is used because it can be used as

DOI: 10.4324/9781003280323-3

a means for transforming both the content and purpose of history as well as the focus of history itself; it can open up new areas of inquiry; it can break down barriers between teachers and students, between generations, between educational institutions as well as the outside world; it can give back to the people who made and experienced history, through their own words (3). Because of its transformative powers, oral history can bring people closer together, forming lasting friendships while providing a wide array of services (9). In this sense, veterans oral history has the potential to challenge assumptions and accepted judgments of scholars by recognizing previously ignored, silenced, and marginalized groups of people. Veterans oral history can be transformative while also changing the social message (Horowitz 617). War "highlights the essence of oral historical work, contrasting the public history of war, of victorious nations, with private tragedies" (Coffman 582). Military oral history captures a range of information, from ordinary experiences to otherwise unobtainable documentation. Oral history with war veterans is a synthesis of the two worlds that soldiers experience: hindsight of the present to recreate the past (Smith 17).

The significance of this work is grounded in the cross-disciplinary and interdisciplinary nature of oral history with war veterans, and at the core of this intersection is how oral history both represents and promotes human values. Oral history, in its very form, affirms that human experience is a matter of preserving life as much as it is a matter of preserving "lives" and human existence cannot be silent, nor can it be nourished by false words but only by true words, with which men and women transform the world. Human beings are not built in silence, but in word, in work, and in action-reflection. It is able to reconstruct – or, in Aristotle's term, "imitate" – the reality of experience, at least as well as any other literary genre can (Bennett 3–5, Freire 69). Oral history permits a discussion of all the troubled issues concerning war, in the voices of ordinary people, within the frame of the personal experience of individual narrators and brings the war and its impact to the human level necessary for comprehending something as chaotic as war (Brinker 16).

Military Oral History

There is a difference between what will be presented in this book for conducting oral history with soldiers and veterans and how the military uses oral history to not only document but also record experiences with veterans. Because of the growing interest in oral history about wars and the military experience, a multitude of interviews with veterans are now available in archives, research institutions, collections, and local and state historical societies and groups. Even presidential libraries have oral histories with military content. Since World War II, every military branch: the Army, Navy, Air Force, and Marine Corps historical offices; government agencies; and universities have collected thousands of oral histories from veterans. More than sixty libraries, including Columbia Center for Oral History Research, have oral histories related to the Navy and Marine Corps. East Carolina University, where my "Breaking the Silence" oral history project originally began in 1999, has more than a hundred such oral histories (Coffman 582). The military initially starting using oral history to document military strategies and battle records but later began creating their own archival documents. For instance, *The Military Oral History at the Virginia Military Institute* (VMI) was originally an initiative of VMI's John A. Adams '71 Center for Military History and Strategic Analysis. The Center's first Director, Dr. Kip Muir (served 2002–2011) initiated the oral history program, in which VMI cadets interviewed veterans as part of their military history classes coursework. The Center continues to see a significant advantage in involving VMI cadets as interviewers, in archival research, in conference presentations, and in publication. Cadets use oral history techniques as part of their classroom work, for capstone and independent research projects, in prize competitions, and for summer internships.

To understand the importance of oral history in military history, Roger Horowitz, in "Oral History and the Story of America and WWII," discusses how oral history helped in society's understanding of the military, political, and social aspects of that war era (617). World War II interviews marked the beginning of accepting oral history as a reliable and trustworthy source, though it was not the first time that journalists or historians ask war participants about their actions and service. Edward Coffman, in "Talking Military History: Reflections on Doing Oral History and Military History," continues to discuss that over two and half millennia ago, the Athenian general Thucydides talked with participants of the Peloponnesian War before writing his history of it. In the early nineteenth century, Lyman C. Draper, a collector of trans-Appalachian frontier manuscripts, interviewed veterans of various frontier wars. He deposited his interview materials in the State Historical Society of Wisconsin. Two American World War I war correspondents, Frederick Palmer and Thomas M. Johnson, used their conversations with war participants as sources for their books (583–584). Samuel L. A. Marshall is most commonly associated with the use of oral history during World War II. As a World War I veteran and *Detroit* newspaper journalist, he became a staff writer after returning to the army. He was a staff officer in the Pentagon when he was tasked to create a better manner in which to describe and analyze small unit actions during battle. During the invasion of Makin Atoll in November 1943, Marshall relied on his journalistic skills to determine the facts of the story – he started asking questions of soldiers who witnessed the invasion. He went a step further by talking to all the survivors of a platoon as a group about what had happened during the battle. He continued to use this approach when he talked with groups of paratroopers after D-Day as well as with other soldiers in World War II, the Korean War, and the Vietnam War (583–584). While Marshall was influential in the Army and later became a brigadier general, after his death in 1977, other scholars questioned his group interview approach as well as some of the assertions he made about men during battle in one of his books. His books, however, did vividly portray the combat experience by utilizing oral sources. However, Forrest C. Pogue became a much more significant person in oral history than Marshall.

Forrest C. Pogue was drafted into the military after he earned a doctorate in history. His oral history career began in June 1944 on a transport ship off the coast of Normandy, France, as he interviewed wounded soldiers from the beach. His career as a civilian historian with the Army continued after the war. He interviewed nearly a hundred Allied and American officers for his book (*The Supreme Command*, Office of the Chief of Military History, Department of the Army, 1954) on Dwight D. Eisenhower's headquarters and included these interviews in the bibliography, before this became a common practice among historians. Pogue was authorized as the biographer of Army General George C. Marshall, commissioned by the Marshall Foundation because of his expertise as an oral historian and his willingness to interview the general at length over several years (Allison 54–55). The military established its own procedures and interviewing strategies in order to obtain the information they needed. For example, the oral history section of the *Marine Corps History Division* consists of an estimated 350,000 interviews with a large percentage of the collection preserved in digital formats. Three oral history approaches used in 1965 as an element of the overall division:

1. **Operational interviews**: conducted in the field and onsite; they provide an immediacy, detail, and accuracy often lacking in interviews conducted with veterans years after the event. The events discussed are not yet in the public record but will eventually become history. These interviews supplement the command chronologies that units are required to submit. They provide the human perspective and experiences that cannot be captured on paper. Operational oral histories are a vital ingredient of the overall mix that goes into writing the official Marine Corps version of combat operations.
2. **Issue-related interviews**: a type of operational oral history, but instead of combat, here the focus is on innovations in technology, doctrine, tactics, or procedures. Other topics that issue-related interviews document include humanitarian operations, contingency deployments, and important training exercises – essentially anything that could be construed as historically significant.
3. **The distinguished Marine/career life histories**: in-depth, detailed, and cover the prominent officer's entire career. These individuals provide valuable insight and perspectives on changes in the Marine Corps and bear witness to important operations in which they have participated. The career interviews are fully transcribed, edited, and indexed. The "smooth" transcript, often with photographs and supporting documents added, is copied, bound, and distributed, with copies going to other military research facilities and appropriate civilian libraries. When completed, the career interview is a most worthy product and widely used, both because the polished transcript is easy to use.

Interviews are welcomed from any individual or organization, and collected interviews are available at the Oral History Office at the US Marine Corps History Division.

Veterans History Project

The Veterans History Project at the Library of Congress (VHP) is vital to practicing oral history with military and war veterans because its creation emphasized the importance and significance of documenting not only the wartime experiences of veterans in our communities but also those experiences of others when their soldiers were deployed. According to VHP website, the project was initiated on October 27, 2000, by the American Folklife Center of the Library of Congress is considered one of the most significant volunteer oral history projects since the Works Progress Administration during the Great Depression. At the time Congress voted unanimously for legislation to create the VHP, which complements the holdings of the American Folklife Center, which was created in 1976 "to document, preserve and present all aspects of traditional culture and life in America. It maintains the largest repository of traditional cultural documentation in the U.S." VHP was an excellent way for Americans to engage in their own history in a very personal manner. VHP's initial goals were to collect audio and videotape recordings as well as letters, diaries, maps, photographs, and home movies. Since its inception, this national collection includes men and women veterans of World War I (1914–1918), World War II (1939–1946), the Korean War (1950–1955), the Vietnam War (1961–1975), and the Persian Gulf Wars (1990–1995), who served in war and in support of combat operations from all military branches of service – the Army, Navy, Air Force, Marin Corps, and Coast Guard. This initial collection also included the Merchant Marines, men and women involved in home front efforts and citizens who supported the armed services, such as war industry workers, United Service Organization (USO) workers, flight instructors, and medical volunteers.

The VHP's initial goals were: (1) to stimulate the opportunities for public learning, by inviting, advising, and supporting individuals and groups to participate; (2) to engage veterans, military, history, educational, and civic organizations as partners to identify, interview, and collect documents from war veterans and those who served in support of them; (3) to preserve and present the collected materials to the public, through the Library of Congress's exhibitions, publications, public programs, and websites; (4) to identify veterans oral history programs and archives; to recognize and work with them to expand the VHP initiative; and (5) to create a comprehensive, searchable, and national catalog of all oral histories and documents collected as a result of this project.

Fifteen years since VHP's inception, wartime demographics changed as the number of living World War I veterans drastically declined. According to the National World War II Museum website, it is estimated that by 2036, there will be no living veterans of World War I. VHP now documents and collects the wartime experiences of the Afghanistan and Iraq Wars (2001–present) and has an interactive website and database in which one can search by keyword, name, war, military branch, state of residence, race, ethnicity, theme, or collection. The VHP also allows anyone to access the collection as well as contribute their own veteran stories. It has now collected oral history narratives from World War I to the Iraq

War. VHP has also produced the book, *Voices of War*, a Library of Congress exhibit, "From the Home Front to the Front Lines," and a play at the American Place Theater in New York. It exemplifies the numerous ways in which veterans oral history is utilized by various communities.

Some of the challenges that faced VHP during its inception are often typical issues that are becoming more common when conducting oral history and designing and planning projects and collections. VHP made a conscious decision not to include the word "oral" in its title, not to de-emphasize recorded experiences but rather, to include a variety of sources, such as letters, diaries, journals, memoirs, photographs, and two-dimensional artwork as representative accounts of wartime experiences in addition to oral histories. VHP also wanted to include accounts of the deceased, those who are too aged or sick to be interviewed. In the early stages, VHP accepted multimedia collections without a concrete idea of how to catalog the various audiovisual formats, manuscripts, and photographs. They did not set a definitive timeframe for the collection or the duration of the project so it was simply assumed that the work being conducted by VHP would be open-ended. Urgency was placed on collecting the World War II experiences, and even though they were aging rapidly, they were still the largest group of living veterans at this time. In this regard, building the collection took priority over any long-term planning. Since VHP was a volunteer effort, they did not expect participants to use high-end audiovisual equipment, so all recording formats were accepted in the beginning. Even with the availability of the Field Kits and guideline instructions, photocopies rather than originals of documents such as photographs and manuscripts were contributed and could not be accepted. VHP was also concerned about the public having quick access to the collection but was challenged with both digitizing the collections and making them available online.

Between 2004 and 2005, VHP gained more visibility and popularity with its publication of two collected book volumes. With continued support from Congressional involvement, VHP eventually reassessed policies for collecting and accompanying digitization. They became selective about accepting older formats like microcassettes and VHS tapes. They began to digitize these formats in large quantities and so had to set firm quality guidelines that were very similar to those of the American Folklife Center and the Library of Congress, such as declining to accept interviews shorter than thirty minutes. VHP also had to outsource large numbers of audio and video materials for digitization. They had to find new storage space for the numerous audio and video files that needed to be transcoded to formats for public access. VHP became a model project for others to follow. They encouraged collaborations with communities, organizations, individuals, and institutions to increase the collections of veterans oral history. Along with the Oral History Association, VHP has established guidelines and procedures that help further this process. In Chapter 8: Project Design and Preparation, Chapter 9: Recording Techniques, and Chapter 10: "Interviewing Techniques," I will refer to VHP's recommendations for forms, equipment, and questionnaires for use when practicing veterans oral history. As one of the primary organizations and databases for veterans oral history, VHP offers the best samples for forms that to use as templates for your own project. Barbara Sommer's *Doing Veterans Oral History* (a publication of the Oral History Association in collaboration with the Library of Congress Veterans History Project) offers additional information and tips for anyone conducting veterans oral history.

Another rather large veterans oral history program is the *Vietnam Center and the Sam Johnson Vietnam Archive* at Texas Tech University. The mission of the Vietnam Center at Texas Tech University is to support and encourage research and education regarding all aspects of the American Vietnam experience and to promote a greater understanding of this experience and the peoples and cultures of Southeast Asia. Anyone can participate, whether an American veteran, a former ally or enemy of the United States, an anti-war protester, a government employee, a family member of a veteran, etc. The archive's mission is "to collect and preserve the documentary record of the Vietnam War. The first collection received by the archive – a package of letters from a Navy hospital corpsman to his family while serving in Vietnam – symbolizes our commitment to preserve the record of individuals and provide greater understanding of their experiences. The archive has collected millions of pages of material and tens of thousands of photographs, slides, maps, periodicals, audio, moving images, and books related to the Vietnam War, Indochina, and the impact of the war on the United States and Southeast Asia."

International veterans oral history organizations are committed to the same mission as VHP. In Canada, *The Memory Project*, an initiative of the Historica Canada, the Canadian Heritage and Veterans Affairs Canada, is a bilingual project connecting veterans and Canadian forces personnel and provides an opportunity to tell their stories through community forums and in classrooms with Canadians. It has also documented Canada's participation in global conflicts, including World War II and Korean War, through oral interviews, digitized artifacts, and memorabilia. *The Imperial War Museums – United Kingdom* houses collections for official and military purposes as well as personal responses to eye-witness experiences of war such as diaries and letters that cover all aspects of twentieth- and twenty-first-century conflicts that involved Britain, the Commonwealth, and other former Empire countries. *The Australian War Memorial's* Oral History and Recorded Sound Collection is a collection that consists of oral history recordings, music, radio interview, and programs that focus on Australia's involvement in war and armed conflict with more than over 5,000 items (over 7,000 hours) of recordings in this collection.

This chapter established the origins of and differences between military and veterans oral history which can be helpful to new and seasoned oral history practitioners as it relates to project design, preparation, and overall project goals.

Bibliography

Allison, Fred H. "We Listen to What Marines Say: The Marine Corps Oral History Program." *Marine Corps Gazette,* June 2005, pp. 54–55.

Bennett, James. "Human Values in Oral History." *The Oral History Review* vol. 11, 1983, pp. 1–15.

Brinker, Williams J. "Oral History and the Vietnam War." *Magazine of History* vol. 11, no. 3, 1997, pp. 15–19.

Coffman, Edward. "Talking Military History: Reflections on Doing Oral History and Military History." *The Journal of American History* vol. 87, no. 2, 2000, pp. 582–592.

Freire, Paulo. *Pedagogy of the Oppressed*. New York: Continuum, 1996.

Frye, Amelia. "Reflections of Ethics." *Oral History: An Interdisciplinary Anthology*, edited by David Dunaway and Willa K. Baum. Walnut Creek, CA: Altamira Press, 1997, p. 162.

Horowitz, Roger, "Oral History and the Story of America and WWII." *The Journal of American History* 1995, p. 617. DOI: 10.2307/2082191

Marine Corps History Division. www.usmcu.edu/Research/History-Division/. Accessed November 7, 2021.

Smith, Clark. "Oral History as 'Therapy': Combatants' Accounts of the Vietnam War." *Strangers at Home: Vietnam Veterans since the War*, edited by Figley, Charles R. and Seymour Leventman. New York: Brunner/Mazel, 1990, pp. 9–34.

The Australian War Memorial. www.awm.gov.au. Accessed November 7, 2021.

The Imperial War Museums–United Kingdom. www.iwm.org.uk. Accessed November 7, 2021.

The Memory Project. www.thememoryproject.com. Accessed November 7, 2021.

The Military Oral History at the Virginia Military Institute. https://digitalcollections.vmi.edu/digital/collection/p15821coll13. Accessed November 18, 2021.

The Veterans History Project at the Library of Congress. www.loc.gov/vets. Accessed November 7, 2021.

Thompson, Paul. *The Voice of the Past: Oral History*. New York: Oxford UP, 2000.

Vietnam Center and the Sam Johnson Vietnam Archive at Texas Tech University. www.vietnam.ttu.edu/virtualarchive/. Accessed November 7, 2021.

3

PERSONAL CONNECTIONS TO VETERANS ORAL HISTORY

Personal Connections

My work with Vietnam Veterans was perhaps predestined. The last American troops withdrew from Vietnam on March 29, 1973; I was born the very next day (which is now the official "Welcome Home Vietnam Veterans Day"). As the daughter of a Vietnam Veteran, I was constantly seeking answers to questions about the war and the profound silence that engulfed my family. My introduction to veterans oral history emerged from my personal journey and led to more than two decades of working closely with military personnel and veterans, on both a personal and professional level. When I was thirteen years old, I discovered an old diary and collection of photographs that were hidden away in the back of my parents' bureau, documents that were reminders of a time that my father, Louis "Smiley" Raynor, never talked about with his family after he returned home from Vietnam. Although he did not object to me reading the diary and looking at the photographs, he was not ready to talk to his young daughter about war. He served with the Third Squad/Fifth Cavalry, nineth Infantry Division (Black Knights) in the US Army. His Military Occupational Specialty (MOS) was Track and Wheel Recovery.

After being drafted and entering the military in 1966 at age eighteen, he started writing in a small, leather-bound burgundy diary measuring 5.5″ × 4″ which was compact enough for him to keep it either in his footlocker or inside his uniform wrapped in plastic to protect it from rain when he was out in the field. Inside the front cover of the diary, he wrote his name, rank, unit, date of departure for Vietnam, body measurements, home address, telephone number as well as the name of his girlfriend who was later to become his wife and my mother. The diary reads according to the dates of his tour of duty from September to December and then the diary continues from January to September. Instead of counting the days of his tour in chronological order, from Day 1 to Day 365, he does a backward

DOI: 10.4324/9781003280323-4

countdown, indicating his first day in Vietnam as Day 365 and to his last day in Vietnam as Day 1.

As my father's tour-of-duty was ending, he wrote the last few days as multiple entries on the same page. He continued to count down until Day 1, September 24, 1968, which was the only blank page in his diary. On several pages in the back of the diary, he wrote the names and addresses of family and friends. On the inside back cover of the diary, there are tiny, monthly calendars for the years 1967 through 1972, where he marked the days of his time in Vietnam.[1]

A year of my father's life, 1967–1968, that he buried in silence until I started digging for that man that my mother so fondly remembered dating before he left for Vietnam, was photographed, and written about in his diary that is now over fifty years ago. For his service in Vietnam and thirty-six months in the US Army, he was awarded the National Defense Service Medal, Vietnam Service Medal, Vietnam Campaign Medal, and Army Commendation Medal. Because of a disagreement with a superior officer, he did not receive the Bronze Star or Purple Heart because he was considered insubordinate. Even after he was wounded in a gas explosion while recovering a damaged armor personnel carrier (APC), he continued active duty. He was honorably discharged on September 7, 1969, at the rank of SP/5 (E5).

I lived with my father's silence about the war for several decades. As a child, I often wondered what happened to him during that war that could create such a profound and deafening silence.

After years of being curious about my father's wartime experiences in Vietnam and intrigued by the stories of other Vietnam Veterans, I was introduced to Wallace Terry's definitive work, *Bloods: An Oral History of the Black Experience in the Vietnam War*. In the introduction of *Bloods*, Terry commented about his intentions for this collection. He wanted to give voices to those Black soldiers who fought in the war that "destroy[ed] the bright promises for the social and economic change in the Black community" (xiii). For Terry, as a reporter for *Time* magazine, covering this story in Vietnam seemed more important than reporting on the civil rights movements at home because Vietnam was "the war of [his] generation" (xiv) and it was dividing a nation. Interestingly enough, the testimonies in *Bloods* represent them as productive citizens of their communities until the war began. They were either faced with the decision to enlist, or they could wait until they received draft orders. Terry felt compelled to tell the story of the young men who called themselves Bloods.

These were not the typical young Black soldiers. They were the new soldiers who replaced the "professionals who found in military service fuller and fairer employment opportunities than blacks could find in civilian society, and who found in uniform a supreme test of their black manhood" (xiv). Terry states:

> These new soldiers were draftees who were just steps removed from marching in the Civil Rights Movement or rioting in the rebellions that swept the urban ghettos from Harlem to Watts. All were filled with a new sense

of Black pride and purpose. They spoke the loudest against the discrimination they encountered on the battlefield in decorations, promotion and duty assignments. They chose not to overlook the racial insults, cross-burnings and Confederate flags of their white comrades. They called for unity among Black brothers on the battlefield to protest these indignities and provide mutual support. A representative cross-section of the Black combat force. Enlisted men, non-commissioned officers, and commissioned officers. Soldiers, sailors, airmen, and Marines. Those with urban backgrounds, and those from rural areas. Those for whom the war had a devastating impact, and those for whom the war basically was an opportunity to advance in a career dedicating to protecting American interests. All of them had a badge of courage in combat.

(xiv–xv)

Even though he made a case for the type of soldier that fit the Blood image, he also made an additional case for representing all Black soldiers who fought in Vietnam, and the combat soldier seemed to be Terry's representative ideal of the Black soldier. He proclaimed, "in any Black soldier of Vietnam can be found the darkness that is at the heart of all wars. What the Black veteran illuminates in these pages of his own humanity as well as racial perception will help complete the missing pages of the American experience and add to the pages of universal understanding of man's most terrible occupation" (xvi).

Even though for many years Terry's collection was accepted as the testimonial truth about the Black experience in Vietnam, but particular oral history collection left me with more questions than answers. I was wondering where were the voices and stories of those young black soldiers like my father, uncles, and cousins who perhaps did not fall into the category of being a Blood, those young men from rural, small-town American who also answered the call of the draft and served their country for various reasons.

The stories in Terry's collection were at times accused of being exaggerated and fabricated war stories that did not represent a universal truth for all black soldiers. Many of the testimonies in the collection weave truthful war experiences with flights of fancy. Because of their marginalization in American society prior to their military service and their harsh treatment during their military service, the veterans possessed a strong desire to become heroes or warriors – if not in their own realities, then in their own stories, during their time of combat and once they returned home. The testimonies shared several common factors but the most fascinating were how they all created the mythological warrior image, both good and bad, and how they managed to evoke the sympathy and understanding of the reader. Both scholars and historians have been questioned Terry's authorial intent of making Black participation in Vietnam a political and racist issue with the publication of selected oral histories and asking why many of the testimonies seemed to mythologize the Black soldier in incomprehensible ways. His universal depiction mythologized the Black soldier and intentionally omitted those who did not represent that warrior image he wanted to portray. Terry's original intent for publishing *Bloods* seemed to have been undermined by his political agenda to paint the entire Black war experience has a racial war that contributed to destroying not only the image of the Black male identity in America but also the hope for a promising future for the Black community. For Terry, the Vietnam War became cultural and racial genocide for not only a Black American servicemen but also for Blacks in America.

Terry's collection became representative of the Black experience before, during, and after the war. What did captivate me about this collection was that Terry's authorial intent was to make America confront its amnesia about Black participation in the Vietnam War due to overt racial prejudices. Upon its publication *Bloods* made two significant impacts. First, it made America confront its collective amnesia about the participation of Blacks in Vietnam and evoked sympathy for those Black servicemen who were disenfranchised before their involvement in Vietnam and further alienated when they returned home. Second, it also, unfortunately, mythologized Black Vietnam Veterans as invincible warriors, thereby creating a cloud of darkness that already had them engulfed in silence. The collection fed society's curiosities about the Black soldier in Vietnam, and it confirmed those myths perpetuated by other wars. The very country they defended, and more specifically, the Black community rendered the veterans silent by not accepting them. So, the collection raises the question: did the veterans reveal the truths of their wartime experiences or did they decide to simply tell the stories that America wanted to hear, thereby creating fabricated images of the Black soldier as good or bad?

I am not contending that my initial veterans oral history work was an extension of Terry's because there are many oral history collections that can fill the gaps since *Bloods* was first published; however, the collection did encourage me to explore various wartime experiences of Black Vietnam soldiers who chose to tell the stories that the nation had not heard before, perhaps more personal stories that evolved from evoked memories years after their service ended. I wanted to document those stories of men and women with whom I was familiar, those in my family and local communities that are often not included in the national experience of war.

My interest grew into a lasting curiosity that led me to seek out my father's story through the voices and experiences of other war veterans. For over two decades, I have been practicing veterans oral history through my own projects and community advocacy work. Though my academic home is in a university department of English literature, I slowly transitioned from simply publishing articles about my preferred literary theories and authors to taking a more thematic approach to how I read the literature within the context of trauma and how the narrative was often fragmented by the context in which the characters found themselves. I soon saw the influence my work with veterans had on everything else I did, from writing to teaching. I decided to stay within a space in which silence, trauma and narrative co-existed and began to work in a manner that could help me explain the context in which a person's voice, and in turn their story, becomes fragmented by lived experiences. For soldiers, that fragmentation was a direct result of war. For some literary characters, it could be any plot twist but often, it was still traumatic circumstances. Toni Morrison's work, which was the focus of my master's thesis, demonstrated for me how a soldier or veteran can be both the protagonist and antagonist of every story written while still being central to the functionality of their families and communities. She, in most of her novels, created spaces in which a soldier/veteran could exist, whether broken, fragmented, or whole, could share the perplexities of their existence after war while still searching through the trauma and silence for some peace, reconciliation and healing. Morrison introduced me to the power of storytelling and how those stories, once shared especially in oral traditions, could manifest a remarkable result. My struggles with writing this narrative are like what I believe author Zora Neale Hurston (or the belief of her critics) also saw as a dilemma with ethnographic work: to present the oral culture of a group on a "manner" best understood by the dominant culture or preserve the essence. The emotion and the complexities of such orality in the same unconventional manner by which they came into existence. After years of living with these stories, I was often perplexed about how to present them. My desire is to be seen in this process as Hurston is seen in *Mules and Men*, "as both observer and observed, as narrator in overly autobiographical writing" (Domina 197). My goal is to capture the essence of storytelling but how is this accomplished through narrative writing? And what is reflective about this process? I had already succeeded in becoming a part of the group of Vietnam Veterans that I was observing, so writing this narrative – telling their stories – how do I stay true to their stories and voices. It was through oral history that I wanted to further explore and to eventually hear my father's stories of war. Most importantly, how can a daughter tell her father's story about Vietnam?

My ongoing dilemma is this: what story is worth telling? What have I learned about my father through the words and images of Vietnam? What lessons did I learn that moved me far beyond the realm of just the war? How did I create a narrative around my father's debilitating illnesses, battles with the VA for accurate benefits and compensation, post-traumatic stress disorder (PTSD)? Why did I inherit my father's legacy of the war?

In order to properly document my father's wartime experiences, I had to first understand the transformative power involved in practicing veterans oral history for both the veterans and the interviewer. It helps us document the otherwise unheard experiences from often marginalized voices while preserving the memories of war and contributing to American military history. Oral history can give war veterans the opportunity to share their own wartime experiences – to finally speak for themselves without being represented by those outside of the war experience.

As a child, I was interested in what happened to my father in Vietnam that forced him to live a life of silence and I also wondered why other veterans were so silent about sharing their own stories. I wanted to explore what I perceived to be the problem: their silence about war. I learned neither the veterans themselves nor their silence was the problem. From their perspective, I was outside their war experiences, so they did not trust me with their memories or stories. In other words, my curiosity was a problem for them. So, the question became: how could I change this? While I was documenting my father's story, I encountered several other war veterans who eventually became my trusted community, participated in my oral history projects, and allowed me to record their stories. They helped me better understand how to gain the trust of veterans by respecting their experiences and protecting their memories and stories. They taught me about their community needs and the special issues involved with working with war veterans. Together, we managed to create and employ strategies and techniques that helped me design and direct two oral history projects while consulting on many others with war veterans and to maintain an ongoing trusted veterans community for more than two decades.

For almost three decades, if I started talking to my father about Vietnam, he would answer my questions, but he never initiated the conversation. Since my father was committed to silence about his experiences in the war, if I wanted to know his whole story, I had to find a way to fill in the missing pieces. I searched for other voices that would help. From that point and throughout my college years, my curiosity about my father's war experiences continued to grow. When I began teaching English literature at East Carolina University, I always incorporated literatures of the Vietnam War into my lessons. When a colleague observed the class and saw how interested and enthused the students were in learning about my father's experiences, his writings and photographs from the Vietnam, he recognized that I had the foundation for a great oral history project. Thus, my project "Breaking the Silence: The Unspoken Brotherhood of Vietnam Veterans" was born. I had previous experience working on a Rosenwald School oral history project, so I was familiar with how oral history could tell the stories of marginalized or forgotten cultures and people, but what I need to learn next was how much care was involved when practicing oral history with a specific demographic.

I wanted my work with veterans to be a collaborative effort. I wanted the participants to help me fulfill the needs of their own community and to help design the project and its products. The focus of my original oral history project was simple: to collect stories of Vietnam Veterans who lived in the eastern regions of North Carolina. These areas had been heavily affected by the draft and many of the veterans, like my father, returned to their hometowns after their service where they have lived for the duration of their lives. I faced several challenges beyond funding, proper equipment usage, interviewing, and time commitment. I was working with a population that rarely, if ever, talked about their war experiences, and I was considered an outsider to their wartime experiences. This work gave me a greater understanding and skill set that is often required when conducting veterans oral history than when conducting an ordinary oral history project because I was documenting experiences that some considered private and personal or shameful and secretive. Regardless of the classification of the memory, I had to learn to handle these memories with care and trust.

First, I wrote and received a grant from the North Carolina Humanities (formerly the North Carolina Humanities Council). Once the project was approved and funded, my challenge was to earn the trust of the veterans and show them that I was sincerely interested in their wartime experiences. In order to connect with the community, I first established a partnership with the Veterans Outreach Center in Greenville, North Carolina. To get the veterans to trust me and my intentions, I spent a tremendous amount of time with those attending centers for readjustment counseling (and therapy) to talk about my intentions with the oral history project. I would show up on weekly just to see if they would change their minds and talk to me, although I got rejected quite regularly.

During one group session in which I was once again talking about my intentions of starting this oral history project because I wanted to learn more about my father's time in Vietnam, they began to tell me why they did not easily trust outsiders. As we continued to talk, I realized that this was not going to be easy because the silence that I thought only belonged to my father about Vietnam, belonged to all of them.

My original project was to focus on the indignities that only Black Vietnam Veterans faced during the war without consideration of other races. This idea was quickly rejected by all veterans of every war and race because they all felt like they had a shared war experience that was larger than individual war and race. They felt there was no point in sharing their experiences with me because they had nothing to say, at least not to me. As I sat in front of those men, on the verge of tears, a World War II veteran began to speak. He encouraged the Vietnam Veterans to participate in the project and share their experiences. He continued to speak about how all the other men he served with had died, and he was one of the few left from his unit and no one ever asked to record his experiences. He reminded the Vietnam Veterans that were also a dying at a younger age than World War II veterans and that this was their opportunity to set the record straight.

Though I explained that my father was a Vietnam Veteran, and he never talked about his experiences with me or our family, the veterans still displayed signs of resentment toward me for attempting to enter their world. I wanted the veterans to understand that this project would provide the world, or at least our community, with answers to years of unanswered questions about what really happened to our soldiers in Vietnam. I explained that I wanted to understand what happened to my father and listening to the stories of these men could help me with the answers.

After I revealed that I was the daughter of a veteran, these men felt even more reluctant to share their experiences with me. One veteran said that there are just certain things that I did not need to know. They wanted to remain silent for various reasons that will be explored later in Chapter 7. At this moment, I began to understand the depth of their silences. They wanted to protect me from the horrors of war because I represented not only the woman/daughter but also the person outside the war experience. They also needed to protect themselves from further alienation by the US government. For both personal and collective reasons, this project was not well received by this group of veterans. I left the Veterans Center discouraged and hopeless about the future of this project. The group leader, Dr. Harold McMillion, told me not to worry because the men would participate but it might just take some time for them to understand the significance of the project and to trust me as an honest researcher and scholar with no intentions of causing them any further stress. What I began to realize at this point is that I needed to gain at least some of that trust that Harold already had with the veterans.

I knew that at this point the focus of the project had to be revised and the project team agreed. After talking with Harold, my father, and other veterans, I understood from our conversations that the generation of Vietnam Veterans I wanted to reach possessed a haunting silence that had to be broken, and the main purpose of the project must provide the veterans with the motivation to talk about their war experiences. The project's sponsoring organization, North Carolina Humanities granted permission to change the title and focus of the project from "The Indignities of War: The Oral History of the African American Experience in the Vietnam War" to "Breaking the Silence: The Unspoken Brotherhood of Vietnam Veterans." Even though the original focus was a fascinating research subject, it would not provide a complete war experience from the local veterans.

The North Carolina Humanities grant provided funds for hiring of project staff. I had students and a few faculty members who were interested in working on this project with me. We were all learning how to do this particular work together, and some team members soon realized that this would not be a typical project that would have a definite start and finish. Once in place, our first task was to build a trusting community. In the second phase, we would conduct the interviews and sponsor a series of public oral history programs. We felt that this plan would provide a comfortable atmosphere for veterans to share some of their experiences with each other, their families, and the general public. We also created a traveling exhibit from diaries, photographs, books, maps, and articles. From February to November 2000, Vietnam Veterans and their families from eastern North Carolina participated as keynote speakers, panelists, or audience members at four community forums. Third, we started interviewing veterans just a year after the community forums began. The project team worked tirelessly to record stories of those willing to participate and who felt comfortable being a part of our project. We initially recorded approximately twenty-five taped oral history interviews with Vietnam Veterans. Within two years of the inception of my oral history project, we began collaborating with the Raleigh (North Carolina) Veterans Outreach Center. The veteran participants helped me further design the next phase of the project specify to what they were willing to do. Instead of focusing on a publication of the collected works, we decided to create educational community forums in which the veterans would have the opportunity to travel throughout the state and share their stories with various communities. They also agreed to allow further documentation of their storytelling sessions. We began receiving numerous invitations to speak in various locations.

The veterans at the Veterans Outreach Center were more receptive of this new focus but my father was still uncertain if he wanted to participate. I wanted him to be involved, but I was not going to pressure him. Because of all the battles with the Veterans Administration (VA) he was fighting regarding disability benefits, I did not want this project to become something that my father despised.

Since I had to gain the trust of the veterans, I decided to sponsor public forums in the community so the veterans could share their experiences with anyone who was willing to listen. The most important aspect of trying to gain their trust was convincing them that there was a community of people who were willing and ready to hear their stories. During the first year of the project, I organized four public forums employing various formats, from keynote speakers to panels and roundtable discussions.

The veterans themselves moderated and ran the forums. They were in complete charge of the atmosphere and the experiences they shared. There was a lively interaction between the veterans and audience members. What was even more remarkable about the forums were the interactions among the veterans at the end of the program. It almost resembled a high school class reunion. The emotions ran very high during the forums because many of the veterans had never talked publicly about their war experiences. As mentioned earlier, their silences protected them from public scrutiny, judgment, and rejection. Finally, this group of Vietnam Veterans knew it was time to debunk the popular myths about them and their war experiences and begin speaking for themselves as well as for those many men and women who did not return home. They were ready to properly tell their own stories – in their own words. Our interviews were a gradual and tedious process, varying with the willingness or resistance and level of trauma of each veteran. Our questions for the interviews were designed to take the veterans back in time to their enlistment or drafting. We wanted them to talk about their tours of duty, their camaraderie with other soldiers, the racial tensions, and some of their most unforgettable memories (see Chapter 15).

Years into the project, a subculture of Black Vietnam Veterans emerged, and this group really emphasized the special issues involved in veterans oral history beyond establishing a trusted community and claiming respect for their traumatic memories and silences. As they continued to tell their stories, they began to talk about the unique experiences of both women and minorities who served. This was not a formal or even expected group. Some of the men attended a veterans outreach center together while others were simply related to each other. They soon became friends and decided that they wanted to be a part of my work on a permanent basis. They acted as my teachers and guide during this process because my father was still silent about his time in Vietnam, so they helped me understand why. They began to tell me about PTSD and how counseling helped them better understand what was happening to them after war. They also taught me a lot about the VA medical system, so I had a different foundation to build my oral history project on because their struggles as well as the best memories of their service was often intertwined in these conversations.

Initially my own doctoral dissertation, "Shattered Silence and Restored Souls: Bearing Witness and Testifying to Trauma and Truth in the Narratives of Black Vietnam Veterans," was not well received by the graduate faculty in my literature and criticism program. While some professors questioned the literary intent and nature of my dissertation project within traditional English studies, a handful of others saw the importance of the work. Given my community fieldwork with local Vietnam Veterans, my dissertation focused on the intersection of race, trauma, silence, and the inherent therapeutic value of storytelling. These concepts were very relevant and important to the veterans oral history methodology. This methodology involved more than just recoding, videotaping, documenting, archiving and preserving their stories. Because practicing oral history with veterans is so closely aligned with trauma, it moves the work beyond the limitations and boundaries of tradition oral history. My decision to focus on a subculture that emerged from "The Breaking the Silence" project helped better focus the work and emphasize the issues of community support and friendship after war. Since the future generations have responded well to the use of oral history within the classroom, educators at all levels are organizing course curriculum, service-learning, and individual and collective projects about the experiences of war veterans.

The most fascinating stories they told were never recorded because these were moments that we were building trust and I worked hard to pass their test. After spending time with this core group of vets my father started to attend an outreach center for therapy and readjustment counseling, and he finally participated in an oral history interview though he was reluctant at first to sit for an interview with me. Once I understood more about who veterans are most comfortable sharing experiences with, I realized that my father, if interviewed, did not want to say or share anything with me. He felt that the interview could change the way I felt about him, so a project team member agreed to conduct the initial interview with my father. During the project, we tape recorded approximately twenty-five interviews on standard cassette tapes, realizing that the community forums took precedence and those interviews helped with the story-sharing events.

By 2007, I wrote a second grant, "Soldier-to-Soldier: Men and Women Share Their Legacy of War," also funded by North Carolina Humanities and would move beyond the Vietnam War and include veterans of other wars. Working closely with several war veterans helped me expand on the original oral history collection and discover a methodological process (with a similar premise as the first project) that becomes unique to their communities which is what is highlighted throughout the book.

My project progressed from simple tape-recorded interviews to videotaping and sound recordings, it continued development throughout the digital age. It was not just my decision to continue the project and expand it beyond diverse platforms, but it was also a decision of the veteran participants, with the understanding that their documented interviews would no longer sit on a shelf or just exist in an archive but would be accessible via the Internet, public radio, film, television, and the public realm in general. With their agreement, I sought out opportunities and collaborations that would move my project into the future. While digital recording was a new concept to some of the older veterans, they realized its importance as a connection to younger generations. Their stories and experiences have a digital and visual presence that transform our assumptions and understandings of war and how it impacts those who served.

Although my veterans oral history projects have been ongoing since 1999, they have evolved tremendously in the last few years, from simple taped-recorded interviews with Vietnam Veterans who had never spoken publicly about their service into a multidimensional, transmedia intergenerational project. In 2016, I collaborated with the Wake Forest University Documentary Film program and *The Imagination Project* on another veterans oral history project, *The Silence of War*. This project, which includes documentary fieldwork leading to the production of the enhanced e-books focused on stories of their personal, social, and political experiences through personal diaries and writings, current speaking engagements on college campuses, and short films that range from biographical pieces to observational sequences about how they cope with PTSD and how their friendships bring them together for life's small and large events. The e-books contain portions of the veterans' wartime diaries and writings, period photos and film as well as contemporary short films about these eight men who met each other decades after serving in Vietnam. The project includes: undergraduate and graduate courses, faculty–student collaborations, documentary fieldwork that is initiated and designed by students, intergenerational relationships between students, faculty, and veterans, web presence through enhanced electronic books and websites, partnerships, and collaborations with veterans outreach centers, veteran panel discussions and forums, short documentary film, academic articles, grants, and veterans outreach assistance.

Now after two decades of practicing oral history with military and war veterans, listening and documenting their stories and experiences, I decided to create a digital space for some of the work to be viewed and shared with others. The evolution of my veterans oral projects is the foundation for this book and the website, "When Writing Goes to War: Stories from Black Veterans of North Carolina."[1]

Note

1 "When Writing Goes to War: Stories From Black Veterans of North Carolina," www.writing-goestowar.com

Bibliography

Domina, Lynn. "Protection in My Mouf": Self, Voice, and Community in Zora Neale Hurston's *Dust Tracks on a Road and Mules and Men*." *African American Review* vol. 31, no. 2, 1997, pp. 197–209.
Wallace, Terry. *Bloods: An Oral History of the Vietnam War by Black Veterans*. New York: Random House, 1984.

II

Issues Common in Veterans Oral History

4
BEST PRACTICES AND ETHICAL GUIDELINES IN VETERANS ORAL HISTORY

I have spent a great deal of time contemplating the best way to address ethical issues of working with military and veterans oral history. Military personnel and war veterans may have all experienced an aspect of life involving fear and violence that many civilians have never witnessed. How could I communicate with oral historians the best practices for working with military and war veterans, and survivors of trauma. I came to realize that working with war veterans unfolds more organically than it might when working with other groups. Sometimes it is hard to follow a project timeline, because the veteran must call the shots. It may take time – a lot of time – to develop the kind of relationship necessary for a serious, compassionate interview. It happens only when a veteran tells you a story and it touches you deeply that you want to hear more. You are not initially thinking about a full-developed project, consent forms, timelines, or what this one story might turn into, but you may sense there is a possibility for this veteran's story to become much more.

These oral history projects can spring from books you read, programs you attend, and movies you see. Some event – a visit to a museum, a mention of a battle, a casual conversation in the grocery line, the name of a soldier or nurse recalled, a location, a photograph, an old letter that you have read, or even a time period that you want to explore – will light a spark for a project. Within these small trigger points may be the root of a larger veterans project. I have found it difficult to just sit at my desk and plan an entire veterans oral history project. The thought process often involves several moving pieces that all seem to be going in different directions at the same time. Therefore it is important to pay careful attention to special circumstances or issues that may arise when. In this chapter, I will provide you with an overview for conducting such interviews once you decide that you are ready.

DOI: 10.4324/9781003280323-6

Interviewer Self-Care

When we pretend there is nothing going on inside of us that is influencing the research and interpretation, we could prevent ourselves from using an essential research tool so the following are some questions that came up for me during my own project that helped keep me balanced during this difficult interviews:

1. Why am I doing this project in the first place?
2. What are the effects on me as I go about this research? How are my reactions impinging on the research?
3. What am I feeling about this (veteran-interviewee)?
4. What group outside the process am I identifying with? (Yow 67)

Best Practices for Oral History With Veterans

Best practices are guidelines, often developed by acknowledged professional organization, for communities of interest to conduct their work thoughtfully and ethically withing the framework developed by their peers in the profession. In this section, I have adapted the Principles and Best Practices of the Oral History Association with guidelines of the Veterans History Project of the Library of Congress for a list of guidelines specifically for doing oral history among veterans. Remember, the guidelines are simply a road map for you to use in your own work with veterans.

Pre-Interview

1. Whether conducting their own research or developing an institutional project, first time interviewers and others involved in oral history projects should seek training to prepare themselves for all stages of the oral history process.
2. In the early stages of preparation, interviewers should contact an appropriate repository that has the capacity to preserve the oral histories and make them accessible to the public.
3. Oral historians or others responsible for planning the oral history project should choose potential veterans based on the relevance of their experiences to the subject at hand.
4. To prepare to ask informed questions, interviewers should conduct background research on the person, topic, and larger context in both primary and secondary sources.
5. When you are ready to contact a possible veteran, oral historians should send via regular mail or email an introductory letter outlining the general focus and purpose of the interview, and then follow up with either a phone call or a return email. In projects involving groups in which literacy is not the norm, or when other conditions make it appropriate, participation may be solicited via face-to-face meetings.

6. After securing the veteran's agreement to be interviewed, the interviewer should schedule a non-recorded meeting. This pre-interview session will allow an exchange of information between interviewer and interviewee on possible questions/topics and reasons for conducting the interview, the process that will be involved, and the need for informed consent and legal release forms. During pre-interview discussion, the interviewer should make sure that the narrator understands:

   - the oral history's purposes and procedures in general and of the proposed interview's aims and anticipated uses.
   - his or her rights to the interviews including editing, access restrictions, copyrights, prior use, royalties, and the expected disposition and dissemination of all forms of the records, including the potential online or electronic distribution.
   - that his or her recording(s) will remain confidential until he or she has given permission via a signed legal release.

7. Oral historians should use the best digital recording equipment within their means to reproduce the narrator's voice accurately and, if appropriate, other sounds as well as visual images. Before the interview, interviewers should become familiar with the equipment and be knowledgeable about its function.
8. Interviewers should prepare an outline of interview topics and questions to use as a guide to the recorded dialogue.
9. Maintain respect for the veteran through full transparency.
10. Be clear about the purpose of the interview and the veteran was asked to participate.
11. Inform the veteran about the final product from the interview and where it will be housed and how its contents will be used in the future.
12. Do not make promises to the veteran that you cannot keep.
13. Take the time to establish trust with the veteran narrator.

Interview

1. Unless part of the veterans oral history process includes gathering soundscapes, historically significant sound events, or ambient noise, the interview should be conducted in a quiet room with minimal background noises and possible distractions.
2. The interviewer should record a "lead" at the beginning of each session to help focus his or her and the veteran's thoughts to each session's goals. The "lead" should consist of, at least, the names of veterans and interviewer, day and year of session, interview's location, and proposed subject of the recording.
3. Both parties should agree to the approximate length of the interview in advance. The interviewer is responsible for assessing whether the veteran is becoming tired and at that point should ask if the latter wishes to continue. Although most interviews last one hour, if the veteran wishes to continue those wishes should be honored, if possible.

4. Along with asking creative and probing questions and listening to the answers to ask better follow-up questions, the interviewer should keep the following items in mind:

    • interviews should be conducted in accord with any prior agreements made with narrator, which should be documented for the record.
    • interviewers should work to achieve a balance between the objectives of the project and the perspectives of the interviewees. Interviewers should fully explore all appropriate areas of inquiry with interviewees and not be satisfied with superficial responses. At the same time, they should encourage veterans to respond to questions in their own style and language and to address issues that reflect their concerns.
    • interviewers must respect the rights of interviewees to refuse to discuss certain subjects, to restrict access to the interview, or, under certain circumstances, to choose anonymity. Interviewers should clearly explain these options to all interviewees.
    • interviewers should attempt to extend the inquiry beyond the specific focus of the project to create as complete a record as possible for the benefit of others.
    • in recognition of the importance of oral history to an understanding of the past and of the cost and effort involved, interviewers and interviewees should mutually strive to record candid information of lasting value.

5. The interviewer should secure a release form, by which the veteran transfers his or her rights to the interview to the repository or designated body, signed after each recording session or at the end of the last interview with the veteran.
6. Recognize when the veteran is finished talking for the time being but be willing to continue the process when the veteran is ready, avoid frustrations, and allow the veteran those moments of silence, privacy, anonymity, and neutrality.
7. Remember to never interrupt or question how the veteran remembers his/her wartime experiences as it relates to dates, names of battles and locations, those they served with, etc.
8. Take a brief note and address it after the actual interview is complete, if an interviewer notices any discrepancies during the interview.
9. Always allow additional time for follow-up questions and perhaps a second interview.

Post-Interview

1. Interviewers, sponsoring institutions, and institutions charged with the preservation of oral history interviews should understand that appropriate care and storage of original recordings begins immediately after their creation.
2. Interviewers should document their preparation and methods, including the circumstances of the interviews and provide that information to whatever repository will be preserving and providing access to the interview.

3. Information deemed relevant for the interpretation of the oral history by future users, such as photographs, documents, or other records should be collected, and archivists should make clear to users the availability and connection of these materials to the recorded interview.

4. The recordings of the interviews should be stored, processed, refreshed, and accessed according to established archival standards designated for the media format used. Whenever possible, all efforts should be made to preserve electronic files in formats that are cross-platform and nonproprietary. Finally, the obsolescence of all media formats should be assumed and planned for.

5. In order to augment the accessibility of the interview, repositories should make transcriptions, indexes, time tags, detailed descriptions, or other written guides to the contents.

6. Institutions charged with the preservation and access of oral history interviews should honor the stipulations of prior agreements made with the interviewers or sponsoring institutions including restrictions on access and methods of distribution.

7. The repository should comply to the extent to which it is aware with the letter and spirit of the interviewee's agreement with the interviewer and sponsoring institution. If written documentation such as consent and release forms does not exist, then the institution should make a good faith effort to contact interviewees regarding their intent. When media become available that did not exist at the time of the interview, those working with oral history should carefully assess the applicability of the release to the new formats and proceed – or not – accordingly.

8. All those who use oral history interviews should strive for intellectual honesty and the best application of the skills of their discipline. They should avoid stereotypes, misrepresentations, and manipulations of the veteran's words. This includes foremost striving to retain the integrity of the veteran's perspective, recognizing the subjectivity of the interview, and interpreting and contextualizing the narrative according to the professional standards of the applicable scholarly disciplines. Finally, if a project deals with community history, the interviewer should be sensitive to the community, taking care not to reinforce thoughtless stereotypes. Interviewers should strive to make the interviews accessible to the community and where appropriate to include representatives of the community in public programs or presentations of the oral history material.

9. Respect the veteran's decision to refuse to be interviewed or have the interviewed shared with others once it has been recorded.

10. Never record a veteran in secret or without consent.

There are a few other guidelines and best practices that should be considered when working specifically with war veterans.

About Consent

Informed consent refers to a conversation/notification with the interviewee, where a representative of the oral history project explains the purpose of the oral history, in particular the role and the rights of the interviewee throughout the project.

In ideal circumstances informed consent consists of both a verbal conversation between the interviewer and the interviewee along with the opportunity to ask questions, to be followed by a written statement of the same. The written statement should document that the interviewee has been given all the information necessary to decide about whether to participate in the oral history project. The interview process must be transparent, with ongoing participation, consent, engagement, and open discussion among all parties, from the first encounter between interviewer and interviewee to the creation of end products. Informed consent plays a key role in ensuring transparency. According to *The Oral History Association (OHA)* consent forms should contain basic yet necessary information, such as the name and date of the interview, name of interview or organization conducting the interview, the purpose/reason for the interview, where the completed interview will be housed, and a statement that the veteran is volunteering to participate in an interview. The consent form should be clear, concise, and transparent. Neither informed consent nor consent forms cover copyright.

The copyright for the information obtained in an oral history interview belongs to those who participated in the interview unless those rights are transferred in writing. The legal release agreement form is used to clarify oral history copyright and to provide guidelines for preservation and future access. All forms are typically signed at the beginning of each interview. In some situations, a veteran may want to proceed with the interview and sign the forms at the end. New forms should be signed for each interview conducted. Sometimes it is best to revise any deed of gifts and/or consent (release) forms that specifically permit digital, electronic reproduction of the interviews to include the possibility of the interviews being shared through the Internet. You should also notify veterans, or if deceased, their closest living relative, before placing the interviews on the Internet. You can also prepare transcripts in formats convenient for the Internet. There are exceptions when family members interview their loved ones who served in wars, the idea of obtaining consent and copyright with a signed legal form may be off-putting to the veteran and end up building barriers rather than trust. If it is clear to the family that the interview will never be made available on the Internet (such as YouTube), published in a book, or be deposited to a library, the family may decide to forego this step.

When to Consult an Expert

Oral history interviewers are usually not doctors, psychologists, lawyers, correctional officers, or trauma workers, yet sometimes veterans need the intervention of these experts. The interviewer's job is to create a safe and inviting environment for the veterans to tell his or her story for the historical record. Because veterans may be vulnerable when discussing war experiences, interviewer training should include the signs when the veteran may need additional help. For example, certain questions during the interview could trigger a traumatic memory and cause discomfort. Consult an expert when:

1. The veteran experiences discomfort or anxiety or emotion associated with a specific memory.

2. The veteran wants to stop the interview and/or asks to see or speak with a family member or a doctor
3. When the interviewer feels unprepared to deal with the veteran's responses to questions.
4. Always contact to an expert to handle libel suits, falsification of information, violations of guidelines, or rescinding of gifts/deed, etc.

Early in my work, another oral historian suggested that I work through a veterans counseling or outreach service as I was learning more about the diverse issues related to practicing veterans oral history (see Chapter 5) as well as post-traumatic stress disorder (PTSD) (see Chapter 6). I decided to work with the local veterans outreach center in which trained counselors who were accustomed to listening to veterans' experiences and knew who to respond in the incidents of discomfort. During my first oral history project, I sponsored public forums so the participating veterans could share their stories and experiences with the community. During these programs, I asked the counselors from the veterans outreach center to facilitate the storytelling issues so they would know when to avoid triggering questions, when to take a break during the storysharing sessions and when the veterans were ready for the programming to end. The veterans felt comfortable with the counselors and would talk more openly and honestly about their experiences. These counselors became an important part of my project staff and were available at various times throughout the process. They helped the interviewers remember their roles and responsibilities (Chapter 10).

Bibliography

Oral History Association. www.oralhistory.org. Accessed November 7, 2021.

The Veterans History Project at the Library of Congress. www.loc.gov/vets. Accessed November 07, 2021.

Yow, Valerie. ""Do I Like Them Too Much?" Effects of the Oral History Interview on the Interviewer and Vice-Versa." *Oral History Review* vol. 24, no. 1, 1997, pp. 55–79.

5

RACE, CLASS, ETHNICITY, DIS/ABILITY, AND GENDER IN THE MILITARY (AMONG VETERANS)

Overview of Demographics in the Military

Groups of marginalized populations were, and still are, subject to different kinds of discrimination – each group and everyone within the marginalized group, in each period of time – has their own story. These experiences were rarely, if ever, formally documented (or acknowledged). The *only way* that stories of marginalized groups in the military can see the light of day is through *oral history*. Project designers and interviewers should keep in mind that policies and general consensus toward marginalized groups changed over time so one cannot assume, for example, that African American soldiers who served in Afghanistan would have the same experience as their fathers who served in Vietnam or their grandfathers who served in World War II. All of this creates a treasure trove for oral historians where oral history is the most useful – individual testimonies of those who never were and never will be documented in the public record.

While the Department of Defense has three military departments: Army, Navy, and Air Force; however, there are six armed service branches. The Army exists as its own department; the Navy and Marine Corp are with the Department of the Navy; and the Air Force and the newly established Space Force (in 2019) are within the Department of the Air Force. The Coast Guard, while considered a military service and branch of the armed services, is actually a part of the Department of Homeland Security. The Coast Guard functions predominately like a law enforcement agency even though it can deploy on missions with the Navy and Marines. There are seven military reserves: Army National Guard, Army Reserve, Navy reserve, Marine Corps Reserve, Air National Guard, Air Force Reserve, and Coast Guard Reserve ("Demographics of the US Military").

Since federal agencies categorize race as American Indian, Asia, Black or African American, Native Hawaiian, or Pacific Islander and white and ethnicity, being

DOI: 10.4324/9781003280323-7

distinct from race, is categorized as Hispanic or Latino and NOT Hispanic or Latino. These categories contribute to the various numbers of enlisted servicemen and women across service branches and genders. Since Hispanic is considered an ethnicity and not a race, it overlaps with all racial categories when examining the racial and ethnic demographics within the military. In 2018, across all military services, minority representation is higher among females recruits than male recruits, while Black men and women are underrepresented among Marine Corp recruits. The Marine Corps has an over-representation of Hispanic men and women recruits. The Coast Guard has the highest portion of white male and female recruits of all the military services. While the officer ranks are similar in racial diversity (as the general population), racial diversity decreases significantly among the higher ranks of the military; generals and admirals are disproportionately white. There is much greater ethnic disparity in the top ranks as well.

While the military does not collect gender information, they do, however, collect consistent information about race and ethnicity in their investigations, personnel databases, and military justice. This could be perceived as limiting their ability to collectively assess data that could identify disparities in incidences that involve racial, ethnic, or gender groups. Despite rank and/or education, Black and Hispanic service members in every branch of the armed forces are more likely to be "investigated, receive nonjudicial punishments like Article 15 or be court-marshaled for such violations of the Uniform Code of Military Justice," according to a 2019 Government Accountability Office report. Given the limited data collection by the military, stories, and experiences of racial and gender bias, discrimination and stereotyping may only be shared during oral history interviews in which they feel comfortable doing so are asked very specific questions along these lines or are participating in a project dedicated to specifically document these experiences.

Stories highlighting some of these issues are included throughout the book in various case studies as examples of projects that focused on racial, gender, and ethnic as well as those that that intersect with dis/ability and socioeconomic and class issues.

The Human Factor: Diverse Issues in Veterans Oral History

According to the Oral History Association's *Principles and Best Practice*, "oral history practitioners must be sensitive to differences in power between the interviewer and the narrator as well as divergent interests and expectations inherent in any social relationship. These dynamics shape all aspects of the oral history process, including the selection of people to interview, research questions, personal interactions during the interview, interpretations, decisions on preservation and access, and the various ways that the oral history might be used."

Here are just a few reminders about practicing veterans oral history, as you make the connections to practicing military and veterans oral history while also considering the many diverse issues related to race, class, ethnicity, dis/ability, and gender. Sarah Loose reminds us that oral history is fundamentally a narrative act, made up of stories that are shared and often interpreted or re-interpreted by the interview-ees, sometimes as a mode of persuasion and/or communication. It, however, differs from other forms of general storytelling and autobiography because of the active role an interviewer plays in helping to share the narrative, preparing questions for the inherent dialogical process, and the longer format that documents the person's experiences. Oral history can also offer "narrative spaces" for those once perceived as different by allowing them to create a holistic portrait of themselves and their story. It helps facilitate a "humanizing" process in which stereotypes are challenged. Also, the oral history interview's expansive and flexible nature allows the narrator to create a framework to conceptualize their own experiences "within a broader socio-political and historical milieu and in the process more fully represent the many dimensions of their identity" (237). Oral history can help reveal various forms of oppression and injustices which may exist in a person's life or community. Alessandro Portelli argues that what distinguishes oral history from other forms of storytelling, fieldwork and interviewing is "the combination of the prevalence of the narrative form on the one hand, and the search for a connection between biography and history, between individual experience and the transformations of society, on the other" (24–25).

Veterans oral history can help with understanding the history of communities and/or issues as well as the causes of contemporary problems. It is often the only format in which the histories of marginalized communities and social movements can be documented and made accessible, particularly in cases where people and communities cannot, do not or will not interact with written texts. Veterans oral history can also de-mystify the process of organizing for social reasons – what worked and did not work in the past. Veterans oral history can provide insight into an individual worldview, value system, and historical consciousness as well as wider processes and moments of transformation that can further social movement build-ing and support organizers by providing access to how individuals make sense of their history and the world.

When differences such as race, class, gender, power, equality, geography (region), age, sexuality, privilege, and dis/ability are present during an interview process, they must be addressed directly and honestly. For example, Norkuras insists:

> When interviewing someone from a different racial or ethnic background, the listener [interviewer] must be sensitive to issues of normative whiteness, racially charged language and difference in experiences. [Interviewers] who engage in oral history interviews about difficult dialogues, particularly, about race, need to learn to talk with someone who is racially different.
>
> *(64–66)*

When practicing military and veterans oral history, it is essential to remember and recognize that each interviewee, even if they are of the same cultural and/or social group, will remember the war in different ways. Conducting oral history inter-views with war veterans may present special issues relating to gender, age, ethnicity, race, socioeconomics, politics, trauma/post-traumatic stress disorder, dis/abilities, silence, and general comfort and familiarity which may affect the actual interview. Donald Ritchie discusses how differences in age, race, gender, socioeconomics, and ethnicity may influence both the questions being asked and the answers given by the interviewees, and for veterans being interviewed, this could also extend to the branch of service and rank. There are no set formulas or prescriptions to overcome these differences, however, you may want to closely match the interviewer and interviewee to qualities they have in common. This could make the veteran-interviewee feel more comfortable. Prior to the starting the interview, the interviewers could help make the interviewee more comfortable by talking a little bit about themselves, looking for commonalities such as where they were born or live, family makeup, school, or work. This kind of person-to-person engagement could help cut across barriers (36–39).

Race and Ethnicity in Military

The Oral History Association's Principles and Best Practices encourages interviewers to work to achieve a balance between the objectives of the project and the perspectives of the interviewees. They should be sensitive to the diversity of social and cultural experiences and to the implications of race, gender, class, ethnicity, age, religion, and sexual orientation. They should encourage interviewees to respond in their own style and language and to address issues that reflect their concerns. Interviewers should fully explore all appropriate areas of inquiry with the interviewee and not be satisfied with the superficial responses. Issues of race and ethnicity may present themselves during the interview process when the veteran is sharing a racial or discriminatory experience. Some groups of people, especially minorities and women, may have been adversely affected by circumstances before and after the war and are considered special groups because, according to Brende and Parson, "the uniqueness of their readjustment needs, have significant gender role and cultural elements. This uniqueness is based, essentially, on their marginal status in American society" (125). Their memories may be difficult to discuss and even share, depending on the war era and the historical context in which they occurred. As the interviewer, be aware and knowledgeable of these types of events, incidents or even atrocities during that particular war; be aware of the racial and political climate in the United States when the veteran was fighting abroad because any upheaval at home could have had a great effect on them during the war. For examples, major incidents that happened at home during a soldier's service may also affect the content of their interviews, for example, the assassinations of Martin Luther King, Jr., President Kennedy, and Malcolm X during the 1960s could have a tremendous effect on what type of war experiences are shared. For example, the veteran's race may have affected the way they were treated, how they were ranked or what types of honors they received. According to Brende and Parson, Black Vietnam Veterans must deal with three challenges to their readjustment: (1) their identities as Black Americans – descendants of slaves; (2) the stigma of having served in Vietnam; and (3) the adverse psychological effects of combat stress (PTSD) (144). Another example happened during and immediately after World War II, when a disproportionated number of Japanese Americans served in the US military, with an estimate of 33,000 in service and approximately 800 being killed in action. A majority of Japanese Americans served in the segregated 100th Infantry Battalion and the 442nd Regimental Combat Team, while others served as translators and interpreters for the Military Intelligence Service. Their service, like many other racial and ethnic groups, was an avenue to upward mobility and the expectation of obtaining citizenship rights previously denied them ("Japanese Americans in military during World War II").

By 2020, men represented 82.8% of active-duty military personnel while women represented 17.2%. Racial minority groups comprised 31.1% of the active-duty personnel and Hispanic or Latino ethnic groups comprised 17.2% of active-duty personnel. Interestingly enough, while 87.9% of active-duty personnel members are located within the United States and US Territories, only four states have the highest percentage of active-duty members: North Carolina, Virginia, Texas, and California. While Hispanics are the fastest growing population in the military, making up 16% of all active-duty military; however, they only comprise 8% of the officer corps and 2% of general/flag officers ("2020 Demographics Profile of the Military Community").

According to "A History of Military Service: Native Americans in the U.S. Military Yesterday and Today," from Native American service women in the Army Nurse Corps in World War I, the Native Americans Navajo Code Talkers in World War II to the 42,000 Native Americans who volunteered to serve in the Vietnam War, Native Americans served in every major conflict for more than two hundred years. They also have served at five times the national average the US Armed Forces. During World War I, approximately 15,000 Native American men, along with several Native American women served, even though they were not yet American citizens. The Indian Citizenship Act that granted citizenship to Indian Nations was not passed until 1924 yet they chose to join the armed forces. By World War II, 800 Native American women served in various branches such as WACS, WAVES, Women Marines, SPARSs, and WASPs. Approximately 10,000 more women would join the Red Cross. During World War II, approximately 45,000 of the 350,000 Native Americans living in the country at the time, enlisted in the Armed Forces, which made them the demographic with the highest rate of voluntary enlistment throughout the entire war.

Today, Native American women serve at a much higher rate than all other demographics with almost 20% of all Native American service members are women compared to almost 15% of all other demographics of service women. Like Native Alaskans, Native Americans continue to serve at a higher rate than any other demographic in the entire country. In comparison to the average of 14% of all ethnicities who served, 19% of all Native Americans have served in the Armed Forces.

Existing Veterans Oral History Projects

The Golden Thirteen: Recollections of the First Black Naval Officers

While *practicing oral history with military and war veterans*, I have met many people who also conduct veterans oral history within their communities, for institutions and for familial or personal reasons. On very rare occasions did I encounter someone who worked for a military installation whose passion about veterans oral history moved them beyond the responsibilities of the job itself.

In 2009, I met Paul Stilwell at an Oral History Mid-Atlantic Region (OMHAR) Conference in Washington, DC. After my presentation on how my father's diary and photos from Vietnam influences my work, Paul and I talked for a while and I learned about his job at the US Naval Institute, at the time as the director of their history division. He had also served in the Naval Reserve and was on active duty during the Vietnam War. While Stilwell has several books that evolved from his work at the Naval Institute and even his work history serving on tank-landing ships and battleships, it was his oral history book, *The Golden Thirteen: Recollections of the First Black Naval Officers* that connected well with my own work. After our meeting, he mailed me a signed copy of his book and we kept in touch.

Stilwell's work is extremely important to both military and veterans oral history because while working through the lens of the Naval Institute, he combined the nuances of military oral history with veterans oral history. In 1944, sixteen black sailors started their training at Great Lakes but only thirteen of them became officers, all whose stories were included in the book. In 1970, a reunion was organized for the men who trained together. All the surviving members were contacted and invited to Monterey, California. These thirteen sailors were called the "Golden Thirteen" by Captain Edward Sechrest who was assigned to the Navy Recruiting Command during that time. This reunion helped establish the collective identity of the group and brought attention to their service during the 1940s. By 1986, the training officer at the Great Lakes Naval Training Center created an opportunity for a series of interviews for the surviving members of The Golden Thirteen, Stilwell's book is "the story of the Golden Thirteen, told by the Golden Eight" (xxvi). Dalton Baugh, Graham E. Martin, Samuel E. Barnes, George C. Cooper, John W. Reagan, Frank E. Sublett, Jr. Jesse W. Arbor, and Justice William S. White were the surviving eight men interviewed as a part of the Naval Institute's oral history program. Dennis Nelson, Charles Lear, Phillip Barnes, and Reginald Goodwin were the other non-surviving members whose stories were told by their comrades. Lewis Williams, J.B. Pickney, and A. Alves were mentioned in the book because they were also trained with the Golden Thirteen but did not become officers. Paul D. Richmond, John F. Dille, Jr., and James E. Hair were the three white officers who were connected to The Golden Thirteen were also interviewed. Stilwell reminds us "as valuable as oral history is for preserving recollections of events not included in history books and official documents, it is certainly not infallible. We all know that memory can play tricks on us and that it grows increasingly hazy with the passing of years. Moreover, memories are reflections of the perceptions of a given time. Thus, if individuals perceived an event differently, they will remember it differently" (xxvii). Because Stilwell did not conduct the original interviews, he understood that having additional material, such as documentary records of the group's training, would add value to the interviews as well as being able to ask additional questions. All the men agreed to a second interview with Stilwell in which he was able to ask more informed questions and the group had become more familiar and comfortable with him.

Since Stilwell had to work within the confines of the book, some editorial decisions were important. He decided to emphasize their entire lives rather than just their time at Great Lakes since none of the eight who were interviewed decided on a career in the Navy. He organized the book around three goals: (1) To demonstrate the backgrounds that those veterans brought to their naval service – the experiences that had formed them and shaped their attitudes, the sort of guidance they had gotten from their parents, teachers, and associates, (2) to describe what sort of lives they led after leaving the Navy, (3) to learn more about society's treatment of its black citizens over the years (a by-product of their service) (xxvii), and (4) he also decided to avoid focus on the events of 1944 so as not to retell the same story over again.

As Stilwell remembered, the value in his veterans oral history project and these stories, he indicated, "the surviving members of the Golden Thirteen have indicated in their oral histories that decisions to leave active service were voluntary. Several have remembered that they were offered promotions if they would remain on active duty" (266). Beyond sharing the stories of their collective wartime experiences, their lives beyond the military and their families, the project also revealed background events about the commissioning of the first black officers in the Navy; the building of the community of black officers and their togetherness and their legacy of increasing opportunities for other black Navy officers and enlisted men and women, and the commitment of the Golden Thirteen to still serve the Navy. As Colin L. Powell points out in the book's Foreword, "The Golden Thirteen were not activists. None of them had sought to make history. The Navy's leaders had simply decided that it was past time to bring down the barriers to opportunity in the fleet; and as a consequence, these thirteen sailors were plucked out of their separate lives to learn the ways of officership. Yet from the very beginning, they understood, almost intuitively, that history had dealt them a stern obligation. They realized that in their hands rested the chance to help open the blind moral eye that America had turned on the question of race. This is their book . . . it is not the "story" of the Golden Thirteen, it is not just their recollections of their time in the Navy, but rather their sense of what it was to grow up, to make a living, to be American, and to be black in the middle years of this century" (vii-viii). Stilwell used the powerful words of the veterans oral history interviews and transferred that vividness to the printed page.

The Navajo Code Talkers Oral History Collection

The Navajo Code Talkers Oral History Collection from 1971 is a veterans oral history project featuring a particular group during a particular war. It consists of eight oral histories of the Marine Corps Navajo Code Talkers of World War II. The original collection is housed at the University of Utah Libraries Special Collection and was collected by the US Marine Corp. The oral history interviews are bound in a volume along with photographs of the Code Talkers working during the war.

The actual oral history interviews were conducted by Benis M. French, a representative from the Marine Corp Headquarters at a reunion held in Window Rock, Arizona during July 9–10, 1971. These interviews reflect the various experiences of the Code Talkers because they were located in different places during the war, which spans from 1942 to 1945. The concept for the Navajo Code Talkers came from Philip Johnston who had lived on a Navajo Reservation for many years and thought that the Navajo language could help the war effort because it was mostly verbal, rarely-written, and perhaps could help create a code that "would enable messages to be sent freely over the radio." Top Marine officials first experimented with the initial concept to determine if it worked effectively before it was approved for use. Afterwards, Navajos either volunteered or were recruited for these efforts with approximately 320 working as CodeTalkers during the war. Their work involved "speaking in Navajo but using substitute words for some things, as would a regular code. It was found that the Navajo speakers could put a message into the code, send it, and translate it faster than any other code system bug used at that time." It is believed that the Japanese were never able to decipher the Navajo code. This collection houses oral history interviews with Sidney Benoni, Alex Williams, Jimmy King, Sr., Wilfred Billey, Carl Gorman, Paul Blatchford, John Benally, and Judge W. Dean Wilson.

Their stories revealed the commonality of their use of the Navajo Code for messages during the war but also revealed other intimacies, such as lying about their age so they could serve, being one of the original twenty-nine Code Talkers, running out food and supplies for several days, during service, carrying a bag of corn pollen (which is considered sacred to Navajo), never being offered a promotion for their service, participating in a tribal purification ceremony to purge the mind of war experiences, how some Navajo were rejected as Code Talkers, going AWOL, using the GI Bill to go to college after their service, and staying in the Marines and serving in the Korean War. Other oral history collections focusing on the Navajo Code Talkers are archived at the Navajo Oral History Project at Dine College and Winona State University.

Gender in the Military

It is important to note that when the draft ended in 1973, women represented only 2% of the enlisted forces and only 8% of the officer corps. Those numbers increased significantly between 1970 and 2018, in which women comprised 16%

of the enlisted forces and 19% of the officer corps. Women only accounted about one-fifth of all military services except the Marine Corp in which they comprised 8% of the total. The Army, Air Force, and Coast Guard had a higher percentage of women officers than for enlisted women.

In the Army, women represented 19% of the officers and 14% of the enlisted. In the Navy, women represented 19% of the officers and 20% of the enlisted. In the Marine Corp, women represented only 8% of the officers and only 9% of the enlisted. In the Air Force, women represented 21% of the officers and 20% of the enlisted; and for the Coast Guard, women represented 23% of the officers and 13% of the enlisted ("Demographics of the U.S. Military").

While the US military has a high number of women serving, according to *USO.com*, they still remain only 16% of the total force, with women representing one of every six Americans in uniform, ranging from 8% in the Marine Corp to 19% in the Air Force. The numbers are far less for women in senior leadership. Only six women have reached the four-star rank. According to Reynolds and Shendruk:

> Among enlisted recruits, 43% of men and 56% of women self-identify as Hispanic or a racial minority; overall, female recruits are consistently more racially diverse than the civilian population. In general, the number of women in the military has increased; they constitute 16% of all enlisted service members and 18% of officers. In the Army, there are nearly as many black women (40%) as white women (45%). The Marine Corps is the only service where the percentage of black men is lower than it is in the civilian labor force.

During my project, as a woman interviewing men, my gender shaped the stories that I recorded, documented, preserved, and interpreted. While I met with and talked informally with women veterans, I did not formally interview any. What happens when the critical lens through which oral history is produced becomes blurred by one's gender? I had to learn exactly what my gender represented for these men within the oral history process and how to negotiate that representation in order to establish a relationship between the listener, narrator, and his experiences.

During the interview, the veterans viewed me as the representative other: woman–child (daughter). Women in the military face issues that could be the same and yet very different than men. These issues might include reasons why they served, sexual assault in the military, hygiene issues (such as availability of products), changing rules regarding women's hairstyles, dress/clothing, motherhood, stereotypes and prejudices, war injuries, and post-traumatic stress disorder (PTSD) as it is experienced by women, combat, promotions in service, and issues with authority/facing issues when they are a high-ranking official. These issues also may prevent women from being more open about sharing their wartime experiences.

When Janey Comes Marching Home: Portraits of Women Combat Veterans

One example of a veterans oral history project that gathers first-hand accounts about a specific aspect of war is *When Janey Comes Marching Home: Portraits of Women Combat Veterans*. It also focuses on women at war, their suffering, trauma, and victories. I met Laura Browder during our time together at Duke University for the *Humanities Writ Large Faculty Fellowship*. We were collaborating with the Center for Documentary Studies (CDS) on our military and veterans oral history projects and Browder's exhibit was on display at the Center. She describes the first time she heard a woman describe her deployment in "glowing terms," she was taken aback. During that time she interviewed fifty-two active-duty women soldiers, sailors, coast guard, airmen, and marines across the eastern seaboard, she admits to hearing many surprising details. Browder's original collaboration for this project with photographer, Sasha Pflaeging, was to not only capture the stories but also see the faces of a representative cohort of the women who served in Iraq, Afghanistan, and surrounding regions. The first version of this project was in the form of a gallery exhibit at the Visual Arts Center of Richmond, Virginia.

When Janey Comes Marching Home project explored a new genre of war photography by showing images of women who have experienced combat along with the women's own words about their experiences. This project was designed to show a new dimension to that traditional "flawed or fragmentary representation of women soldier in popular culture" (Browder 10). The oral history interviews revealed various themes. While some were common, the women gave varied responses to the questions. Some of the more common themes were motherhood and deployments, stereotypes about women soldiers as either too masculine or sexually out of control (sluts or bitches), threats of sexual assault, supporting the troops, comradery within units, marriage, sexism, sacrifice, and duty. Browder's original goal for the project was to interview pro-war and anti-war combat veterans. The project received three grants from the Virginia Foundation for the Humanities who insisted on reassurance that the project would not take a position on the current war – that it would not become an anti-war project. Her approach to attract attention was to use letters of introduction to leaders and members of anti-war veterans groups and to distribute her business cards at rallies. This did not work. After doing all the interviews, she realized that "'pro-war' and 'anti-war' [were] not always relevant categories" (10). What she discovered through the project was the women's impressive capacity to survive: "the means they had for balancing their family lives and their military lives and the complex ways they found to keep on going after seeing and experiencing horrific things" (10). Browder's hope for the project was by coming face to face and interviewing and photographing women who had been deployed would help those outside of that experience and culture better understand how women soldiers experienced a long war and how their stories "may ripple out and affect the experience of all women" (10). For Browder's methodology, interviewing active-duty personnel presented some limitations in the interview process. There were some questions that she could not ask. For example, she could not ask about the "Don't Ask, Don't Tell" policies. Also, according to regulations, a public affairs officer had to be present for the interviews, though in reality, one was rarely if ever present. Browder encountered how commissioned officers were trained "to not say anything interesting to representatives of the media." During one particular interview, Browder asked the public affairs officer if she could sit further away from the interview table because it was distracting the soldier being interviewed. At another base, the public affairs officer assisted Browder with setting up the interviews, maybe because she had faced harassment from her commanding officer and had been busted down in rank during her deployment.

Laura and Sascha conceived their collaboration as a way of hearing the stories and showing the faces of some of the first large cohort of women – over 180,000 who had served in the American military in combat zones in Iraq and Afghanistan from all five branches of the military. They debuted an exhibition of forty large-scale (30″ × 40″) color photographic prints, each paired with a narrative panel in the portrait subject's own words at the Visual Arts Center of Richmond, Virginia. The exhibit was later developed into a book by the same name. The photographer's goal was to document these women visually while still close in time to their deployment, their feelings, and emotions still raw and very real. The portraits and oral histories together convey stories that are moving, comic, heartbreaking, and thought provoking. They emphasized the oral history aspect of the project by allowing online visitors to hear these women's voices – to let them speak for themselves. "Though male soldiers have long been the subjects of documentary photographs and oral history interviews, it is rare that women have had a chance to relate their experience of combat. If we listen to them, these women – these mothers and wives, these soldiers and veterans – will unsettle our fixed ideas about Americans at war and add dimension to the often flawed or fragmentary pop culture depictions of women in the military: as novelties, but not as real soldiers. *Janey* is a dramatic portrait of women at war and what they have to say about loss, comradeship, conflict, and hard choices. It sheds light on two conflicts in which women are officially barred from combat in American armed services, and how they engage with the enemy, suffer injuries, and sacrifice their lives in the line of duty. Their stories illustrate how serving in a combat zone is an all-encompassing experience that is transformative, life-defining, and difficult to leave behind." This project was funded by grants from the Virginia Foundation for the Humanities, the National Endowment for the Arts and the College of Humanities and Sciences at Virginia Commonwealth University. The original oral history interviews resulted in a traveling photographic and narrative exhibit as well as a book.

The military does not report data on the LBGTQ+ service members. Prior to the 2010 appeal of the "Don't ask, Don't tell" policy during President Barack Obama's administration, gay, lesbian, and bisexual individuals could serve in the military but were forced to conceal their sexual orientation. In 2016, President Obama allowed transgender individuals to also serve openly in the armed forces but this policy was later reversed by the Trump administration. While the military does not accept transgender recruits, a few exceptions are granted to those who were allowed to enter into the military between the 2016 decision and the reversal of that policy ("2020 Demographics Profile of the Military Community").

Dis/Ability and Class in the Military

When you begin an oral history project involving veterans, you may wonder whether a veteran's disability, injuries, service-connected illness or PTSD affect the interview, or even whether or not he has a visible physical condition. This is a very valid question because any of these issues could affect the interview process in the following ways: length of time, availability, comfortability, location, specific questions about the disability or illness, and/or unexpected interruptions due to the injury or illness. If these are the circumstances, the interviewer may need to travel to visit the veteran in the hospital or other type of facility. As with other veterans, certain aspects about their experiences, disabilities, and illnesses may be off limits for discussion during the interview process. If the veteran shares these issues with you beforehand, you may ask if you can ask about them during the interview. For example, a veteran who is an amputee due to an injury or wound during the war, may not be willing to discuss that particular incident. Also, some disabilities, such as PTSD, are not visible so as an interviewer, you should be aware if the veteran has any particular triggers (see Chapter 6). The interviewer should respect those boundaries. It is also helpful to learn a bit about the disability rating system that the VA uses during their rating and compensation process. Your understanding of this process will also help build more trust between the interviewer and veteran because they will sense that you cared enough to learn more about their circumstances prior to the interview.

Based on their benefits administration, the *Veterans Administration*, a service-connected disability is a disability, disease, or injury incurred or aggravated during active military service. The amount of basic benefit paid depends on how disabled the veteran is determined to be. The VA makes a determination about the severity of the veteran's disability based on the evidence he submits as part of his claim, or that VA obtains from his military records. VA rates disability from 0% to 100% in 10% increments (i.e., 10%, 20%, 30%, etc.). Certain circumstances may warrant receiving additional amounts. These include if the veteran has very severe disabilities or loss of limb(s); the veteran has a spouse, child(ren), or dependent parent(s); and/or he has a seriously disabled spouse. If the VA finds that a veteran has multiple disabilities, the disability ratings are not additive, meaning that if a veteran has one disability rated 60% and a second disability rated 20%, the combined rating is not 80%. This is because subsequent disability ratings are applied to an already disabled veteran, so the 20% disability is applied to a veteran who is already 60% disabled. The disabilities are first arranged in the exact order of their severity, beginning with the greatest disability and then combined with a ratings table that involves intersecting, combining, and calculating the subsequent disabilities to nearest degree divisible by 10. The VA calculates the total service-connected disability rating by combining evaluations of each disability rather than adding the individual ratings together. Conditions that were due to military service but not considered disabling are assigned as 0%.

Here are some other factors to consider when interviewing a veteran with a disability or injury: Try not to bring unwarranted attention to any physical differences. Do not ask outright about the disability, rather offer prompts and let veteran respond if he wants to talk about it. Continue to check in with the veteran during the interview about his comfort and willingness to continue. Remember to be patient with the veteran if more breaks and interruptions are needed to perhaps take medication, grab a snack, or visit the restroom. Also, be willing to stop the interview if the veteran appears to grow tired. It is fine to reschedule the interview to accommodate the needs of the veterans.

Issues related to socioeconomics and politics also may surface during the interview process. Interviewing veterans who were drafted (who served prior to 1973 and involuntary selected for service) may differ than those who enlisted (volunteered for the branch of service in which they preferred to serve) and from those who attended college and then entered the military. As the interviewer, be aware of how economics, politics, and class affected military experiences. Given the socioeconomic background of the veteran, the interviewer may share particular stories that are reflective of being drafted into a particular branch of service opposed to being able to enlist. Some may express strong political views about their service or to their opposition of war in general.

Disposable Heroes: The Betrayal of African-American Veterans

Benjamin Fleury-Stein's *Disposable Heroes: The Betrayal of African-American Veterans* utilizes oral history to emphasize interracial bonds between veterans and economics. Fleury-Stein discusses reflections on his own middle-class white privilege as a veteran of Operation Desert Storm and how perhaps that helped him better deal with his anxiety and challenges after returning home from the Persian Gulf. He compared his experience to the African Americans veterans with whom he served. His oral history was conducted on the premise that "race deeply matters" especially when lives of the veterans are "characterized by a series of interconnected traumatic experiences" such as health disparities and inequalities, employment, housing, education, and criminal justice. This book illustrates how important it is for marginalized veterans, including veterans of color and women, to participate in oral history projects to highlight the need for policy reform by the Veterans Administration.

Fleury-Stein admits that the "rich life history data is the heart of the book. It is a collection of thirty (30) interviews with African American soldiers who enlisted "in the military to escape the ravages of racial segregation and social immobility." These veterans served from the Vietnam War and All Volunteer Force (AVF) era. As the interviewer and oral historian, Fleury-Stein admits, even though he served in Operation Desert Storm, to being ignorant of "the extent to which racial marginality continues to be perpetuated in the African American community in general and in the lives of black veterans in particular." His interviews and research revealed that the men's lives were "characterized by a series of interconnected traumatic experiences (e.g., profound housing inequalities, loss of a loved one, and other health-related crises)."

Fleury-Stein stresses the urgency of these stories and experiences in light of economic inequalities, endless wars, increased incarceration rates, unemployment, and poverty. His objective for the book was to "focus on the post-war experiences of black veterans on their own words. He includes life histories of African American veterans' pre-and post-military experiences. He contends that the interviews provide "historically contextualized situations and conditions" and as a collection of oral histories "present an indictment of a longstanding legacy of dehumanizing social conditions that African Americans have endured for generations. And in the case of black veterans, the combined pains of readjustment into civilian society means continued racial oppression; for Vietnam era veterans it means experiences with overt Jim Crow racial segregation and in the case of AVF era veterans the "New Jim Crow" of white backlash toward integration and mass incarceration.

Fleury-Stein's project began in Fall 2009 at Independence Housing (IH), an all-male temporary housing faculty located in Wilmington, Delaware, which is one of the more impoverished and racially isolated sections of the city. He was told by local Veterans Affairs representatives about the African American veterans actually living in IH, and the initial interviews were arranged by the IH executive directors. Once the initial, multiple life history interviews were completed then the interviews expanded beyond IH to other mostly impoverished, nearly all-black neighborhoods. IH veterans also put the project team in contact with veterans at the Wilmington Veterans Administration. The next series of interviews was completed via snowball sampling that began with informal meetings in the Wilmington Veterans Administration reception area which was known as a popular hangout for black veterans waiting to attend various classes or therapy session. Fleury-Stein arranged several interviews with Vietnam, and AVF era veterans, but by 2010, he struggled to find additional leads to veterans who wanted to be interviewed. After receiving a lead from a Cold War era veteran, he decided to go outside of Delaware to the Baltimore Chapter of the National Association of Black Veterans (NABVETS). He was able to conduct final interviews by telephone with African American veterans of Operation Iraqi Freedom.

The veterans oral history interviews, both in-person and via telephone, were the overall plan for Fleury-Stein's book, which he describes by chapters, from emphasizing the African American veterans as a social problem, presenting the experiences of African American Vietnam and AVF era veterans beyond the "theatre of combat" when the armed forces moved from conscription to voluntary recruitment (post-1973–present) to focusing on how their experiences are evidence of "collective trauma," as defined by Kai Erickson as "gradual realization that the community no longer exists as an effective source of support and that an important part of the self has disappeared" (153–154).

These oral history projects were all or created in different ways and for different reasons but all captured the essence of the veteran experiences after war. Whether the project is well planned and graciously funded or done for very personal reasons for very little money, the finished product can look very different. From elaborate exhibits, audio recordings, journals, books to well-archived artifacts, veterans oral history projects are all based in a similar methodology that pays attention to the needs of the veterans and how best to tell a particular story that best serves and represents their communities and cultures.

Bibliography

"2020 Demographics Profile of the Military Community (Department of Defense)." https://download.militaryonesource.mil/12038/MOS/Infographic/2020-demographics-active-duty-members.pdf. Accessed April 10, 2022.

"A History of Military Service: Native Americans in the U.S. Military Yesterday and Today." *USO, Inc.,* Monday, November 8, 2021. www.uso.org/stories/2914-a-history-of-military-service-native-americans-in-the-u-s-military-yesterday-and-today. Accessed on April 19, 2022.

Alessandro Portelli. *Battle of Valle Giuliano: Oral History and the Art of Dialogue.* Madison, WI: University of Wisconsin Press, 1997.

Brende, Joel Osler, and Erwin Randolph Parson. *Vietnam Veterans: The Road to Recovery.* New York: Plenum Press, 1985.

Browder, Janey. *When Janey Comes Marching Home: Portraits of Women Combat Veterans.* Chapel Hill, NC: UNC Press, 2010.

"Demographics of the U.S. Military." *Council of Foreign Relations,* July 13, 2020. www.cfr.org/backgrounder/demographics-us-military. Accessed April 10, 2022

Fleury-Stein, Benjamin. *Disposable Heroes: The Betrayal of African-American Veterans.* New York: Rowman & Littlefield Publishers, Inc., 2012.

"Japanese Americans in military during World War II." *Densho Encyclopedia.* https://encyclopedia.densho.org/Japanese_Americans_in_military_during_World_War_II/. Accessed June 20, 2022.

Loose, Sarah K. "Oral History for Building Social Movements, Then and Now." *Beyond Women's Words: Feminisms and The Practices of Oral History in the Twenty-First Century,* edited by Katrina Srigley, Stacey Zembrzycki and Franca Icaovetta. New York: Routledge, 2018, pp. 236–243.

"Military Justice: DOD and the Coast Guard Need to Improve Their Capabilities to Assess Racial and Gender Disparities." *Report to the Committee on Armed Services, House of Representatives. United State Government Accountability Report,* May 2019. www.gao.gov/assets/gao-19-344.pdf. Accessed April 26, 2022

Norkunas, Martha. "Teaching to Listen: Listening Exercises and Self-Reflexive Journals." *The Oral History Review* vol. 38, no. 1, 2011, pp. 63–108. DOI: 10.1093/ohr/ohr043. Advance Accessed March 25, 2011.

"Over 200 Years of Service: The History of Women in the U.S. Military." *USO.com.* www.uso.org/stories/3005-over-200-years-of-service-the-history-of-women-in-the-us-military. Accessed November 7, 2021.

Reynolds, G.M. and A. Shendruk, Demographics in the U.S. Military Council on Foreign Relations CNA Population Representation in the Military Services: Fiscal Year 2016 Summary Report, 2018, April 24 www.cfr.org/article/demographics-us-military

Ritchie, Donald. *Doing Oral History. A Practical Guide.* New York: Oxford UP, 2003.

The Navajo Code Talkers Oral History Collection. http://archiveswest.orbiscascade.org/ark:/80444/xv32742. Accessed November 15, 2021.

"Veterans Administration." *U.S. Department of Veterans Affairs.* https://benefits.va.gov/benefits/. Accessed November 7, 2021.

6
TRUST, TRAUMA, AND THE HUMAN FACTOR

Understanding Trauma

According to Leigh Gilmore in *The Limits of Autobiography: Trauma and Testimony*, "trauma, from the Greek meaning, 'wound,' refers to the self-altering, even self-shattering experience of violence, injury, and harm" (6). In *Unclaimed Experience*, Cathy Caruth defines trauma as an overwhelming experience of a sudden or catastrophic event in which the response to the event occurs in the often delayed, uncontrolled repetitive appearance of hallucination and other intrusive phenomena. The experience a soldier faced with sudden and massive death around him, for example, who suffers this sight in a numbed state, only to relive it later in a repeated nightmare, is a central and recurring image of trauma (11).

Dissociation, a complex mental process during which there is a change in a person's consciousness which disturbs the normally connected functions of identity, memory, thoughts, feelings, and experiences, is one way a veteran may deal with overwhelming trauma, according to "What are Traumatic Memories," trauma can lead to extremes of retention and forgetting; terrifying experiences may be remembered with extreme vividness, totally resist integration or a combination of both . . . some aspects of traumatic events appear to get fixed in the mind, unaltered by the passage of time or by the subsequent experience. Veterans may use their natural ability to dissociate in order to avoid conscious awareness of a traumatic experience while the trauma is occurring and for an indefinite time following it. Conscious thoughts and feelings or memories about the overwhelming traumatic circumstance may emerge at a later date.

Mowatt and Bennett discuss how combat-related stress was present and recognized during the Civil War. During that time, it was known as "soldier's heart." During World War I, combat-related stress became known as "combat fatigue" or "shell-shock." After World War II, it evolved into "battle fatigue" or "gross stress reaction"

DOI: 10.4324/9781003280323-8

(288–289). These days we refer to this as post-traumatic stress disorder (PTSD). PTSD was not officially recognized as a diagnosis by the *American Psychiatric Association* until 1980. It was then defined by the Diagnostic Statistical Manual (DSM-V) as "experiencing or witnessing a traumatic event that puts the person's life in actual or threatened danger or a situation that poses a threat to others." PTSD has three prevalent areas: (1) re-experiencing, (2) hyperarousal, and 3) avoidance/emotional numbing. According to the Veterans Administration and the *National Center for Post-Traumatic Stress Disorder*, this can occur after a person has been through a traumatic event, such as combat exposure, child sexual or physical abuse, terrorist attack, sexual or physical assault, serious accidents, or natural disasters. During a traumatic event, like combat exposure, he thinks that his life or others' lives are in danger. The person may feel afraid or feel he has no control over what is happening around him.

Most people have some stress-related reactions after a traumatic event, but not everyone gets PTSD. Brende and Parson define PTSD as the development of characteristic symptoms following a psychologically traumatic event that is generally outside the range of usual human experience. The characteristic symptoms involve re-experiencing the traumatic event, numbing of responsiveness, reduced involvement with the external world, symptoms of depression and anxiety, increased irritability associated with unpredictable explosions of aggressive behavior, hyper-alertness or exaggerated startle response, sleep disturbances, recurring nightmares, guilt about surviving when others have not, guilt about behavior required for survival, memory impairment, trouble concentrating, avoidance of activities that arouse recollection of the traumatic event, and/or feelings of detachment or estrangement from other people (77–78).

It is important for oral historians to understand how trauma and PTSD can affect the veteran's memory of events, including during the interview. Your veteran may have diagnosed PTSD, undiagnosed PTSD, or no PTSD symptoms at all. He may or may not self-identify or disclose this information to you prior to the interview. According to the National Center for Post-Traumatic Stress Disorder, before conducting an interview, you can also familiarize yourself with the symptoms of PTSD: reliving the experiences (re-experiencing symptoms) through bad memories or nightmares, flashbacks in which the person feels as if he is re-living the event again.

1. Avoiding situations that remind him of the event that could trigger memories, so he may avoid talking or thinking about the event, which may manifest itself as silence during the interview.
2. Negative changes in beliefs and feelings, such as the way he thinks about himself and others may change because of the trauma. He may feel fear, guilt, or shame. He may not be interested in activities he used to enjoy, which allows him to avoid the memories.
3. Feeling keyed up (hyper-arousal or hyper-vigilance). He may feel jittery, always on alert or on the lookout for danger. He may have trouble sleeping or concentrating.

4.   Other issues that may stem from PTSD include feelings of hopelessness, shame, and despair; depression or anxiety; employment problems; drinking or drug problems; physical symptoms or chronic pain; and relationship problems including divorce.

Establishing trust with the veteran and/or veteran community early in the process, understanding the nature of trauma and how this may affect memory and the storytelling process is an important aspect of veterans oral history.

Building Trust With the Veterans Community

This issue of trust has been a running theme throughout the book because it is so important in veterans oral history. I spent a tremendous about of time with my core group of veterans by visiting their homes and seeing them in various settings. Others who have worked with me on projects have also done the same, like going fishing, spending time going through old photographs, visiting their farms, or joining them with their hobbies. The trust you take the time to develop when getting to know the veteran will allow you to accomplish the goals and objectives of your oral history project. I reiterate this trust factor throughout the book to remind you to focus on the needs of the veteran community.

Keep in mind that the roles of the interviewer may shift during the course of the oral history project just like they do with any personal relationship. Be open, committed, and willing to negotiate those roles. Use deep listening skills and all the other cues in the veteran's body language and behavior to understand his behavior at any given moment and meet him on his own terms. Be willing to be personal during the interviews, learn the military language/way of speaking to match their speaking style. Most important, be willing to wait for the interview. This requires patience. The veteran will agree to the interview only when they feel you are trustworthy.

Journalist Anderson Cooper wrote in *Dispatches from the Edge: A Memoir of War, Disaster and Survival*, "in the midst of tragedy, the memories of moments, forgotten feelings, began to feed off one another. I came to see how woven together these disparate fragments really are: past and present, personal and professional, they shift back and forth again and again" (5). As you begin to design your veterans oral history project take some time to examine your own beliefs and experience. Use these questions to guide your thinking because they become important as you delve into some of the issues common in veterans oral history:

- What are some of the most meaningful aspects of veterans' narrative storytelling?
- What is my personal experience with war veterans? Think specifically about each of these people: what their war story is and how open they are about it; how much they have told you directly vs. you learning about it another way; and how you might approach them in an interview.

- What is my personal knowledge about minority or gender subcultures in the military? How might I use that knowledge (or ignorance) in working with veterans?
- How well do I understand the importance of narrative storytelling to the healing experience of veterans? (Is narrative – storytelling through veterans oral history a useful therapeutic clinical tool? Do I understand how a veteran's "anniversary reaction" can affect the oral history process?)
- What do I consider the important philosophical and ethical questions that arise when practicing veterans oral history?
- How well do I understand the nature of memory and the nature of trauma? How can I use this information to develop trust in the war veteran I wish to interview?
- Will the veteran consider me "one of them" (based on race, gender, age, experience, military branch or rank)? How can I use this relationship to the best advantage in cultivating trust with the veteran? (there are advantages of both outsiders and insiders in interviewing)
- Do I understand that, that there may be limitations when practicing veterans oral history in developing trust, or simply, in timing? Can I recognize when "enough is enough," when the veteran is unwilling to talk further, and I need to step back?

Understanding trauma and establishing trust with veterans can often help the interviewer better guide the questions asked and evoke specific memories and stories. "Storytelling components order life experiences for war veterans because it provides structure and continuation in order to make meaning of these events – with this process, a coherent personal narrative in which the relationships between different elements of the story are interwoven: subjective truths, interpretations, emotional evaluation, unity, integration, purpose, and meaning. Veterans may process memories with other veterans in therapy/counseling groups of the same war or with others who served with them, while family members were considered as a safe haven that protected the veteran from conversation and memories about traumatic war experiences" (Burnell and Nigel 60). It is imperative that you, as oral historian, understand the effect of trauma on a veteran's memory, which sometimes may lead to silence about the traumatic experiences. In "Voices from Vietnam: Oral History in the Classroom," Patrick Hagopian argues that "every oral history interview takes place in a context and against a background of mutual expectations on the part of the interviewer and interviewee. In any interview, the oral historian must reflect on how those factors shape the narrative."

Anniversary reactions, according to Ellen Hendricksen, also known as trauma anniversary, is the annual remembering or reliving a traumatic moment or event that is specifically timed. It can be emotionally complex and distressing because it is a stark reminder of a moment or experience that one would rather not remember. Familiarizing yourself with the veteran's military service prior to the interview will definitely help if the interview process is interrupted due to an anniversary reaction of something that happened during deployment. Each veteran may experience issues depending on their individual circumstances, so it is best to understand culture, history, medical, economics, social, political, and religious elements of the individual or community you are working with.

Bibliography

American Psychiatric Association. www.psychiatry.org. Accessed November 7, 2021.

Bessel A. van der Kolk, and Rita Fisler, "Dissociation and the Fragmentary Nature of Memories: Overview & Exploratory Study." *Journal of Traumatic Stress* vol. 8, no., 1995, pp. 505–525.

Brende, Joel Osler, and Erwin Randolph Parson. *Vietnam Veterans: The Road to Recovery*. New York: Plenum Press, 1985.

Burnell, Karen and Nigel Hunt. "Coping with Traumatic Memories: Second World War Veterans' Experiences of Social Support in Relation to the Narrative Coherence of War Memories." *Ageing in Society*, 2010, p. 60. DOI: 10.1017/S0144686X0999016X

Caruth, Cathy. *Unclaimed Experience: Trauma, Narrative, and History*. Baltimore: Johns Hopkins University Press, 1996.

Cooper, Anderson. *Dispatches from the Edge: A Memoir of War, Disasters, and Survival*. New York: Harper, 2006.

Gilmore, Leigh. *The Limits of Autobiography: Trauma and Testimony*. Ithaca: Cornell UP, 2001.

Hagopian, Patrick. "Voices from Vietnam: Oral History in the Classroom." *The Journal of American History* vol. 87, no. 2, 2000. DOI: 10.2307/2568766

Hendrikson, Ellen. "5 Ways to Deal with Anniversary Reactions." *Psychology Today*, September 22, 2016. www.psychologytoday.com/us/blog/how-be-yourself/201609/5-ways-deal-anniversary-reactions. Accessed November 7, 2021.

Leigh, Gilmore, *The Limits of Autobiography: Trauma and Testimony*. Ithaca: Cornell UP, 2001.

Mowatt, Rasul and Jessie Bennett. "War Narratives: Veteran Stories, PTSD Effects, and Therapeutic Fly-Fishing." *Therapeutic Recreation Journal* vol. 45, no. 4, 2011, pp. 286–308. www.researchgate.net/publication/285800529_War_Narratives_Veteran_Stories_PTSD_Effects_and_Therapeutic_Fly-Fishing. Accessed November 7, 2021.

National Center for Post-Traumatic Stress Disorder. www.ptsd.va.gov. Accessed November 7, 2021.

"What are Traumatic Memories," Sidran Institute/The Sheppard and Enoch Pratt Health Systems Traumatic Stress Education and Advocacy. 1994 Sidran Institute – Public Service Brochure. www.sidran.org/wp-content/uploads/2019/04/What-Are-Traumatic-Memories.pdf. Accessed November 7, 2021.

7

THE NATURE OF MEMORY AND SILENCE

After many years of practicing veterans oral history, using the interviews as a part of my teaching curriculum and writing about the methodology and value in their stories and experiences, I understood the interconnectedness of trauma, memory, and silence and just how they manifest during the interview process. Walter Benjamin observed that after World War I, men returned home from battle having grown silent and seemed unable to thoroughly communicate their war experiences or even talk about them. The war veteran becomes a historical storyteller who "takes what he tells from experience – his own or that reported by others. And he in turn makes it the experience of those who are listening to his tale" (83–87). Since memory serves to preserve, recover, or liberate us from the past, it has the power to speak to or reconstruct those experiences that were and may never be again. War experiences that manifest themselves into horrific memories can possibly result in distortions, exaggerations, fabrications, and socially and culturally constructed stories. With the nature of memory, the past can be seized only as an image which flashes up at the instant when it can be recognized and is never seen again. For every image of the past that is not recognized by the present as one of its own concerns threatens to disappear irretrievably. To articulate the past historically does not mean to recognize it the way it really was. It means to seize hold of a memory as it flashes up at a moment of danger (Benjamin 255).

According to Judith Herman in *Trauma and Recovery*, traumatic memory that merely repeats the past without consciousness must be transformed into narrative memory because it narrates the past as the past. Once the traumatic memory is narrated, it can be integrated into the veterans' life stories (175–177). Because the veterans have held onto their experiences for so long and have become somewhat uncertain of what they actually experienced, ultimately, this wound of trauma manifests itself as a code of silence thus hindering the emergence of the testimonies

DOI: 10.4324/9781003280323-9

of the veteran's war experiences. War, trauma, memory, and silence permeate the narrative truth that emerges out of their silence.

Jay Winter, who characterizes silence as a performative nonspeech act, the silent performance of the terror, endured during the war. He identified three types of silence:

1. The silence of those who cannot speak, either because the war left them mute, or, more significantly, because they did not think anyone would listen to what they had to say.
2. The silence of those who choose not to speak, either due to gender codes which forbid, especially, men to speak about certain physical and even more so psychological injuries, or due to a general reluctance to relive the past; or to cover up the past for personal or political reasons.
3. The silence of groups, or collective silence, which occurs when a group agrees to not speak about certain subjects either in public or in private, which is not the same as forgetting; just because a memory was silent, did not mean that it was not present.
4. Can only soldiers understand war?
5. And most significantly for this book, how did the things left unsaid by shell-shocked soldiers affect their families, especially their wives and children, who often had to suffer under the violence meted out by their silent, traumatized but undiagnosed, husband or father?

Winter also contends that there exists an essentialist silence, in which the idea exists that only those who lived through an experience can adequately describe or speak about it.

Martha Norkunas in "Teaching to Listen: Listening Exercises and Self-Reflective Journals," asks a very important question: "how profoundly can I listen to another person so that he/she can narrate his or her life story in a way that best reflects his/her life story in a way that best reflects his/her sense of self, and the many layers of meaning embedded in the construction, performance, and content of that narrative" (64)? Given the apparent silences or gaps that are a significant part of trauma stories and "war" stories, how does the interviewer learn to navigate those silence spaces during the interview process with the veteran? When dealing with silence after trauma, Alessandro Portelli reminds oral historians about "listening beyond words," in which one must be aware of the cultural forms and processes by which "individuals express their sense of themselves in history" (ix, xi). The silences become a significant part of their stories – what they are choosing to remember and share versus what they desire to forget and never share. While such factors as race, class, gender, respect, equality, and ability can affect the interviewing process and how best to respond to those narrative silences.

According to Michael Frisch's model of shared authority, the veteran has a role. Frisch argues that the shared responsibility of listener (interviewer) and veteran (interviewee) results in the final interview document. Frisch insists that while editing and interpreting are important to the oral history process, the "act of listening" is the "first moment of creation" during the interview process (71). The interviewer has to distinguish and differentiate silences as a form of communication in which nonverbal expressions, intimacy, and distance, and a way to frame how both thought and speech occur (74). Are the silences intentional moments of reflection, on behalf of the interviewer or is the interviewer inserting the silence into the process? However, silence after trauma functions a bit differently.

Kathryn Basham in "Combat Trauma" discusses the silencing paradox occurs when a veteran seeks understanding and recognition of their experiences but does not want to talk about them. Basham also notes that in the last decade there are waves of service men and women returned home from war zones in Iraq, Afghanistan, and other regions and reintegrated back into their families and communities. More than 50% of all post-deployed US veterans do not seek help (276). They might also believe that civilians – those outside the war experience – cannot fully understand the effects of the experiences so the veteran may resort to silence (291).

According to Dori Laub in "Bearing Witness or the Vicissitudes of Listening," the listener to trauma comes to be a participant and a co-owner of the traumatic event: through his very listening, he comes to partially experience the trauma in himself. The relation of the victim to the event of the trauma, therefore, impacts on the relation of the listener to it, and the latter comes to feel the bewilderment, injury, confusion, dread, and conflicts that the trauma victim feel. He has to address all these, if he is to carry out his function as a listener, and if trauma is to emerge, so that its henceforth impossible witnessing can indeed take place. The listener, therefore, by definition partakes of the struggle of the victim with the memories and residue of his or her traumatic past. The listener has to tell the victim's victories, defeats, and silences, know them from within, so that they can assume the form of testimony. The speakers about trauma on some level prefer silence so as to protect themselves from the fear of being listened to – and of listening to themselves. It serves them both as sanctuary and as a place of bondage. Silence is for them a fated exile, yet also a home, a destination, and a binding oath. To not return from this silence is rule rather than exception. The listener must know all this and more. He or she must listen to and hear the silence, speaking mutely both in silence and in speech, both from behind and from within the speech. He or she must recognize, acknowledge, and address that silence, even if this simply means respect – and knowing how to wait. The listener to trauma needs to know all this, so as to be a guide and an explorer, a companion in a journey onto an uncharted land, a journey the survivor cannot traverse or return from alone.

Survivors did not only need to survive so that they could tell their stories; they also needed to tell their stories in order to survive. There is, in each survivor, an imperative need to tell and thus to come to know one's story, unimpeded by ghosts from the past against which one had to protect oneself. One has to know one's buried truth in order to be able to live one's life (58–63).

Survivors of trauma are urged to testify repeatedly to their trauma in an effort to create the language that will manifest and contain trauma as well as the witness who will recognize it. Thus the unconscious language of repetition through which trauma initially speaks (flashbacks, nightmares, and emotional flooding) is replaced by a conscious language that can be repeated in structured settings. Language is asserted as what which can realize trauma even as it is theorized as that which fails in the face of trauma (Gilmore 7).

PTSD, Silence, and the Nature of Memory

When I was growing up, my father and uncle were always whispering about their time in Vietnam. When I approached them to listen, they immediately fell silent. There were also things that they would never tell me, who for most of them represented someone outside of the war experience. What I originally thought was a secret or something that they did not want me to know was actually silence. For my father, I was always seen as the one outside the war experience: the child and (woman)daughter. Sometimes my mere presence either stifled or intensified the telling of their stories. Sometimes they did not talk at all. These were not secrets that they kept from me; they chose silence.

Harlan Joel Gradin, Scholar Emeritus of the North Carolina Humanities Council and Former Assistant Director/Director of Programs, described my "Breaking the Silence" oral history project like this: "perhaps more than the shared experiences of Vietnam, it is the shared silences, and the very fact of speaking through them, that Sharon's project and this issue explore." When I spent time with Jamaican writer and activist, Dr. Erna Brodber, discussing my oral history work with veterans, she asked, "Once you get people talking, once you turn them on, how do you turn them off"? This was a profound question for conducting oral history with war veterans (that will be discussed further in Chapter 10, Interviewing Techniques), because once they trust you and those memories are triggered, whether they memories are good or bad, you have provided them a safe and comfortable space in which to share their burdens of war. It could be more damaging to abruptly end the interview session before they have finished processing that memory or sharing that particular experience.

The interviewer will bear the burden of the veteran's trauma, experiencing at least part of their trauma during the process. You must also be able to recognize their silence as part of their narrative structure by establishing limits and boundaries that you will cross during the interview (see Chapter 6):

> The listener to trauma comes to be a participant and a co-owner of the traumatic event: through his very listening, he comes to partially experience the trauma in himself. The relation of the victim to the event of the trauma, therefore, impacts on the relation of the listener to it, and the latter comes to feel the bewilderment, injury, confusion, dread, and conflicts that the trauma victim feel. He has to address all these, if he is to carry out his function as a

listener, and if trauma is to emerge, so that its henceforth impossible witness-ing can indeed take place. The listener, therefore, by definition partakes of the struggle of the victim with the memories and residue of his or her trau-matic past. The listener has to tell the victim's victories, defeats and silences, know them from within, so that they can assume the form of testimony.

(Laub 58–59)

I knew not to pressure the veterans to continue to discuss intense moments of trauma. Understanding PTSD and recognizing the veteran's level of readjustment, I respected the fact that they chose silence over voice. First, it must be established how silences can be detected within their stories and if these silences are indicators either of trauma or speech acts. Silences are especially telling when the interviewer is able to recognize them and distinguish their function within the narrative. Rec-ognizing silence as a form of language evolves from the interviewer learning various aspects about listening to the experiences being shared. Dana Jack in "Learning to Listen: Interview Techniques and Analyses," asks, "How do we listen to interviews without immediately leaping to interpretations suggested by prevailing theories?" (165). This often happens when the interviewer has made the conscious decision to remain outside of the experience, both uninformed and unprepared, until invited to share the burden of the experience with the veteran-narrator.

Recognizing silence as a language became a huge factor in my oral history work because within that silence existed a completely new and different story than what was spoken and shared. That was the beauty in the rendering of their stories – never asking narrators for more because their pauses, gaps, and moments of reflec-tion revealed the true story of the war – the real trauma of their experiences, moments in time that could not verbalized. During this process, it became obvious to me that their silence was unique because it was not only individual and personal, but it was also collective. It took years of isolation and adjustment for them to be able to break this profound silence and attempt to make sense of their military service. In their willingness and need to both give voice to their war experiences, they were able to share the truths buried in their memories. They were willing to bear witness to past atrocities and testify to the pain that trauma created in order to shatter their profound silence.

Interviewing veterans can be a gradual and tedious process, varying with the willingness or resistance and level of trauma of each veteran. Interview questions should be chosen to take the veteran back to the time in which he enlisted or were drafted or back to the original story of how he ended up choosing or being drafted in the first place. The questions should encourage them to talk about their tours of duty, their camaraderie with other soldiers, cultural differences, racial politics, gender issues, and some of their most unforgettable memories. It becomes a huge responsibility of the interviewer to record the authentic oral history. Because voice is often privileged over silence, during the interview, the veteran might struggle with the dilemma of pos-sessing the need to talk about their traumatic experiences and desiring to forget those same traumatic experiences.

The Interviewer as Transcriber/Transcribing the Interview

After moving through the interview process, your role as the interviewer may evolve into your role as the transcriber. The rendering the voice to print suggests a kind of permanence, and a suggestion of "authority" when the spoken interview seemed like a conversation/impermanent. When the transcriber is also the interviewer, it may seem like a quantum leap from a private, albeit recorded, conversation to a transcript that will become a part of the historical record.

As transcriber of the veteran's experiences, you may face some difficult ethical decisions. When looking at the function of oral histories, specifically with war veterans, historical preservation for the sake of cultural identity can (must) be considered within various contexts (i.e., the military, local communities, and individual families). The ethics of the oral history may constitute preserving the authenticity of the voices, the language, the culture, the identity and the story being told. Transcribing the interview as it is conveyed becomes just as important as collecting the interview and documenting the life of the veteran.

Donald Ritchie argues that oral historians who document traumatic events find that survivors of trauma will often refrain from talking about those traumatic experiences, even to those people close to them. With the first stage of grief being shock and the second being denial, people can remain in denial for a long time. However, as the survivors grow older and others who shared that traumatic experience dies, the survivors will [may] open up to sharing their memories as a way to reconcile the experience while ensuring that future generations do not forget. There is an ongoing debate among oral historians about the benefits of conducting the interview close to the event discussed, or years after, when the narrator has had the time to reflect and process the memory. In fact, there is no better or worse time, just different. If the oral history project has the gift of time or a family has an ongoing relationship with the veteran, interviews at various points along the spectrum of the veteran's memory can be enlightening, and can reveal, not only the war story but also the veteran's progress in processing the experience. The military pioneered debriefing interviews with soldiers immediately following after a battle or returning home from a tour of duty. These interviews are short and focused. For a nonmilitary interview with soldiers other factors are at work. Even though memories of the events will be sharper closer to the event, veterans may not be ready to share those traumatic experiences of war, especially with those outside of the war experience.

Interviews conducted months, years, and even decades after the event actually gives the veteran more time to reflect on their participation in the event and sort through its significance and how it may have affected their lives (Ritchie 36–37). Winter and Sivan state, "when people comment about the past – their own personal past, their family past, their national past, and so on – they bring with them images and gestures derived from their broader social experience" (6). This broader social experience is often captured in veterans oral history because it becomes a combination of personal, family public and even traumatic memories of their experiences in the military and during wartime.

It has only been recently that silence has been identified as a manifestation of trauma. "Silence and Discourse," Fran Sendbeuler's study of silence and voice, provides a well-established foundation for understanding silence, which is the inability or unwillingness to speak. It also takes the place of the written or spoken word when a traumatic act impedes the telling. Because silence has the power to manifest itself in a variety of ways, connecting silence to the trauma of war veterans can become just as difficult to comprehend as their war experiences. Sendbeuler contends that silence is silence itself, and it is meaning without language; silence can be meaningful, just as language can be without meaning. Silence as a form of discourse occupies a space even more vast than does language, due to the limitlessness and endlessness of silence and all that silence can imply. Beyond her definition of silence, it also allows a place in which more can be said, thereby allowing space for the listener/reader to question that silence in search of a narrative truth. Silence cannot just be categorized as Sendbeuler terms good or bad, "Good silence being that which implies meaning" and "bad silence is repressed silence or that which causes the reader [and/or listener] to understand negation or change in the substance of meaning."

For some veterans, silence functions in multi-faceted manners, depending on the individual veteran and their circumstances. In a broad sense, silence within narratives can function either as a speech act or as an indicator of trauma. Specifically, silence emerges in the testimonies of veterans either when a memory presents itself and they refuse to give voice to it; when they cannot remember the event as it happened and they choose not to speak about it at all; or when they remain silent to protect themselves from ridicule and scrutiny or to protect those who are closest to them, particularly their family members.

My father's silence functioned on all of these levels at different times. Silence becomes the veteran's only self-defense. Because voice is privileged over silence, veterans struggle with the dilemma of possessing the need to talk about their traumatic experiences and desiring to forget those same traumatic experiences. Silence appears in both oral and written narratives when either the act of speaking is interrupted or broken or when something has been either purposely or unintentionally omitted. Silence is also a form of resistance to specific circumstances that later had significant consequences. To those outside the war experience, understanding the war, as outsiders, is completely different than those of the soldiers who fought in it. The difficulty is compounded when those who fought the war are silent. Dori Laub states:

> Silence is for them a fated exile, yet also a home, a destination, and a binding oath. To *not* return from this silence is rule rather than exception. The listener must know all this and more. He or she must *listen to and hear the silence*, speaking mutely both in silence and in speech, both from behind and from within the speech. He or she must recognize, acknowledge and address that silence, even if this simply means respect – and knowing how to wait. The listener to trauma needs to know all this, so as to be a guide and an explorer, a companion in a journey onto an uncharted land, a journey the survivor cannot traverse or return from alone.

(58–59)

The veteran's silences can ultimately become a significant part of their narratives as an inaudible utterance or gesture can become a narrative. Whether we realize it or not, the veterans have two distinct testimonies: the one that they tell – and the other one that exists only in silence. War veterans may render two distinct silences: individual silence and collective silence. They are very protective of each other even when it comes to telling someone else's experiences. It is very difficult for them to speak for other veterans. Most war veterans feel as if their war experiences, if told, could be damaging to those who are exposed to them. They also maintain their individual silence because they do not want anyone to think negatively of them or the acts they committed. The veterans maintain a strict code of silence in order to protect the worlds in which they retreated after the war because they suffered both individual trauma and collective trauma. Their silences protected them from scrutiny and judgment, loss and grief. David Aberbach, in *Surviving Trauma: Loss, Literature and Psychoanalysis*, states, "they mourn family, friends, and the communal bonds which have been violently torn apart; they mourn the cheapening of their lives, their lost dignity and humanity; they mourn all that might have been was not" (2).

Since the veterans are still trying to process and comprehend their own place and purpose in the war, they do not want to suffer at the hands of others who do not or cannot comprehend their war experiences. According to Gilmore:

> Survivors of trauma are urged to testify repeatedly to their trauma in an effort to create the language that will manifest and contain trauma as well as the witness who will recognize it. Thus the unconscious language of repetition through which trauma initially speaks (flashbacks, nightmares, emotional flooding) is replaced by a conscious language that can be repeated in structured settings. Language is asserted as that which can realize trauma even as it is theorized as that which fails in the face of trauma.
>
> *(7)*

Talking with several Vietnam Veterans during my own oral history projects allowed me to discover a process that becomes unique within itself based on varying factors. The following process emerged, almost sequentially, as a result of war veterans being ready to break their silences and share their experiences:

1. The veterans recognize themselves as trauma survivors and not just survivors of war who are possibly dealing with symptoms of PTSD and have begun to identify the stressors of that trauma.
2. They recognize themselves and their experiences as historical memories that have been not only untold but also unrecorded or discredited.
3. They express their willingness to make an attempt to reconcile their two worlds – the one that was before the war and the one that will never exist again.

4. They acknowledge the existence of a willing listener who will help shoulder the burden of the traumatic experience being shared. A certain level of trust must be achieved between the teller and the listener.
5. They possess a willingness to give voice to their historical memories, and as they remember, they also are willing to tell the stories of others with who they served and shared a collective experience.
6. They acknowledge the silences that impede their interviews and experiences but continue to participate in the telling and/or writing of their own experiences by adding their own words and meanings. They are inscribing themselves into the narratives instead of allowing others to speak for them.
7. The veterans recognize the power in both language and silence, but they continue their healing process through sharing their stories with others.

This process varied according to each individual veteran who participated in the project due to their level of trauma and their comprehensibility of their own war experiences.

My father never really talked about his experiences in Vietnam. Instead of telling fanciful stories or stories that evoked sympathy, he remained silent. This decision may or may not have been a conscious one. For years, the source of his silence would be a mystery. Even though I asked him about his experiences on several different occasions, he never obliged me with an answer. His silence became very crippling, emotionally, spiritually, physically, and mentally, not only for himself but also for the rest of our family. It was a difficult transition for my father to move from silence to voice because, for many years, his silence protected him from all those horrors of war. He thought that his silence would also protect his family from those same horrors. But it did not. Early in their relationship, my mother, Katie, was very protective of my father. As his girlfriend before he got drafted into the Army and later, as his wife, when he returned home, she protected his silence.

My parents had their hands full keeping five children in line, but sometimes our father seemed a bit distanced from the children. My mother taught us certain rules about our father that really did not make sense to us, as children, at the time. "Never wake your Dad when he is sleeping, even if he is shaking and sweating. Just let him sleep; the nightmare will end." "Never sneak up behind your father to surprise him. I know how you children like to play." "Do not bring any more Vietnam War movies home to watch." "NO! We cannot have salmon and rice for dinner; Daddy cannot stand the smell." There were just certain rules that we learned to abide by and never questioned. Without knowing it, our way of life centered around our father's war experiences.

For a long time, it seemed as if my father did not have time for us because he was always away from home as a long-distance truck driver. Not only was his invisibility affecting the entire family, but the community also labeled us as the children without a father. An elementary school teacher once questioned my mother about our father, and needless to say, this infuriated my mother. No one seemed to understand the plight of the Vietnam Veteran, nor could they offer any understanding to their families.

I always believed that my father was away because he had to be – that was his job. But as I got older, I realized that my father had unique tendencies when it came to spending time with the family. He would often retreat to a world in which he functioned alone; most of the time, he would go outside the house where he could keep himself busy. What was even more interesting than my father's silence was how my mother remained just as silent as my father about his experiences during Vietnam. It was a subject that was never discussed in our house. We knew that our father had been in a war when he was young, but it wasn't until many years later that we would realize the adverse effect that his time in Vietnam would have on all of us.

Our silence was so overwhelmingly well-kept that my younger sister did not even know that our father was a Vietnam Veteran until she was sixteen years old when she began helping me with the "Breaking the Silence" project in 1999. Our lives were so engulfed in silence that we never realized that the youngest person in the family did not even know what she was being protected from. Even though my father was dealing with the ghosts from Vietnam on a daily basis, we were all guilty of dismissing his trauma as symptoms of his other existing medical conditions. The pain and suffering caused by the war had captured our entire family and held us captive. For years, we were drowning in our own worlds of hurt and silence. Until the start of the "Breaking the Silence" oral history project, we, as a family, never realized how much this code of silence about the war fragmented our family. In the beginning, this profound silence served its purpose because it protected us from the outside world – those who had not been personally touched by the war. Silence also allowed us to laugh and celebrate in times when there was little joy. Our silence had become much more than just the absence of the spoken word; it had become our only means of communicating with each other. We had become a family unable to express certain emotions because of a deep-rooted fear of loss and grief that had manifested itself within us. We only knew how to protect each other, especially our father.

The world had been extremely cruel to not only him but also the rest of us, and as a family we only trusted each other. Until recently, we never thought that in order for us to begin to heal that it was necessary not only for our father to talk about his Vietnam experiences but also for us as family members, to talk about how Vietnam affected us. We decided that we needed to help my father not only endure but also eventually overcome the days and nights of agony that brought Vietnam rushing back into his memories. Trauma affects different people in very different ways, so the depth of the wound left by the traumatic event can only be measured by the survivor's ability to recognize and acknowledge the events and begin the healing process.

I emphasize silence quite a bit because in the midst of working with veterans, I experienced my own trauma. I was the victim of a violent crime and soon afterwards, my life began to change quite drastically. Even though I was still doing the work with veterans, conducting the interviews and planning community forums to share these stories, I had grown silent. My father knew what I had experienced and expressed his concern. He soon shared it with the core group of veterans because he felt like I needed encouragement to address the trauma. During one of our meetings, they staged an "intervention" to encourage me to seek counseling to help me talk through these experiences since I had been their advocate and encouraged them to break their silences. Time passed and I had to revisit the traumatic incident because I had to appear in court to testify to the events. Once the court trial was complete, I once again retreated into silence. I finally took the advice of the veterans and went to counseling. Prior to this, I had only an intellectual understanding of PTSD as it related to war veterans, but I would soon have to gain a deeper insight once I received my own clinical diagnosis of PTSD. I was overwhelmed with the diagnosis because I did not feel as if my experience even compared to those of the veterans. Once I shared this with them, they told me that "now my work can begin." They never saw it as a comparison, but rather as an opportunity for us to help each other cope with our own trauma. These veterans provided me with an instruction manual about how to live a life affected by trauma; how to learn to let go and move beyond what was lost or what has changed; and instead of mourning that loss, learn to live with it and embrace what fear creates. They provided structure for my life once again. I did not quite understand what it meant to live with trauma until I had experienced my own, so soon my own story of trauma started to parallel the work that I was doing with the veterans. My own trauma and PTSD forced me to deal with how it had changed me and who I had become. As I continued to experience a few more unfortunate events, I was reminded of what Anderson Cooper said, "Sometimes I wonder if I'm the person I was born to be, if the life I've lived is the one I was meant to, or if it is some half-life, a mutation engineered by loss, cobbled together by the will to survive" (15). It awakened me to the additional issues of trauma survivors who had lived their lives in silence about their experiences and all the issues that prevented them from sharing those stories with others.

Bibliography

Aberbach, David. *Surviving Trauma: Loss, Literature, and Psychoanalysis*. New Haven, CT: Yale UP, 1989.

Alessandro Portelli. *Battle of Valle Giuliano: Oral History and the Art of Dialogue*. Madison: University of Wisconsin Press, 1997.

Anderson, Kathryn, and Dana Jack, "Learning to Listen: Interview Techniques and Analysis." *Women's Words, the Feminist Practice of Oral History*, edited by Sherna Berger Gluck and Daphne Patai. New York: Routledge, 1991.

Bashma, Kathryn "Combat Trauma." *Trauma: Contemporary Directions in Trauma Theory, Research, and Practice*, edited by Shoshana Ringel and Jerrold R. Bradell. New York: Columbia UP, 2020, pp. 274–311.

Benjamin, Walter. *Illuminations: Essays and Reflections*. Translated by Harry Zohn. New York: Schocken Books, 1968.

Brodner, Erna. Personal interview, 2002.

Cooper, Anderson. *Dispatches from the Edge: A Memoir of War, Disasters, and Survival*. New York: Harper, 2006.

Frisch, Michael. *A Shared Authority*. Albany, NY: State University of New York Press, 1990, pp. xx, 71.

Gradin, Harlan Joel. Personal Interview. "Breaking the Silence: The Unspoken Brotherhood of Vietnam Veterans." *NC Crossroads* vol. 6, no. 2, 2002, p. 13.

Herman, Judith, *Trauma and Recovery: The Aftermath of Violence-from Domestic to Political Terror*. New York: Basic Books, 1997.

Laub, Dori. "Bearing Witness or the Vicissitudes of Listening." *Testimony: Crisis of Witnessing in Literature, Psychoanalysis, and History*, edited by Shoshana Felman and Dori Laub. New York: Routledge, 2000, pp. 57–74.

Norkunas, Martha. "Teaching to Listen: Listening Exercises and Self-Reflexive Journals." *The Oral History Review* vol. 38, no. 1, 2011, pp. 63–108. DOI: 10.1093/ohr/ohr043. Advance Access publication 25 March 2011.

Ritchie, Donald. *Doing Oral History. A Practical Guide*. New York: Oxford UP. 2003.

Sendbuehler, Fran. "Silence as Discourse." Paper Presented at the Meeting of the Group for Early Modem Cultural Studies, Rochester, NY. 1993. www.mouton-noir.org/writings/silence.html.

Winter, Jay. "War, Memory and Silence." *Connecting Memories Research Initiative in the School of Literature, Languages and Culture,* November 8, 2019. http://research.shca.ed.ac.uk/csmch/2019/11/10/jay-winter-war-memory-silence/. Accessed November 7, 2021.

Winter, Jay, and Emmanuel Sivan. *War and Remembrance in the Twentieth Century*. United Kingdom: Cambridge UP, 1999.

III

Conducting a Veterans Oral History Project

8
PROJECT DESIGN AND PREPARATION

A veterans oral history project always begins with an idea – a question about something of historical interest, a contemporary issue that will interest researchers in the future, or an individual person's life story. The previous sections provided an overview of veterans oral history, my personal connection to it, best practices and ethical guidelines, importance of building trust, and how to better understand trauma. Now it is time to focus on planning and conducting your own project. Take a moment to think just what you want to accomplish. From here, you can follow the steps and suggestions to plan and conduct an oral history project involving veterans. A series of forms referenced in this chapter and provided in the Appendix will help guide your thinking. Whether you are considering an oral history with a veteran family member, a series of interviews at a veterans' reunion gathering, or a scholarly life history for a research institution, there are certain steps involved in the planning, interviewing, post-interview processing, and in most cases, sending the interview to a repository (library or archives) for safe keeping. For the purposes of discussion, we will call the series of steps an *oral history project*.

I want to note that the 2020-global pandemic stopped oral historians in their tracks, requiring them to rethink almost every step of project design, interviewing, and the important rapport between the interviewer and interviewee from personal contact. At the time of this writing, oral historians are finding new ways to achieve the quality interviews in a world where the personal contact among us seems unsafe. This chapter will incorporate the emerging best practices for doing oral history in our new world.

Different Approaches to Veterans Oral History Projects

One way to clarify your project in your mind is to ask, who is your intended audience for the interviews. Veterans oral history projects can be loosely divided into three categories, depending how the interviews are intended to be used.

DOI: 10.4324/9781003280323-11

Family Oral History

Many families document their collective history by interviewing family members, including veterans, and capturing memories through their own voices. The narrative of a veteran family member could be recorded as a single interview or as part of a larger family history project. In either case, the interview will be conducted *by* a family member, *with* a family member veteran, *for* the enjoyment of the family in the present and in generations to come. The assumption is a family oral history project is private, and intended for family only. In this case, the interview may be more informal, the questions may be geared toward an insider audience who is already acquainted with the narrator and some record keeping and paperwork, such as legal release forms that may can be dispensed with. Later in this chapter, different cases are provided as examples for the different approaches to veterans oral history projects.

Community Oral History Project

In a community oral history project, a group, such as a church, community organization, or public library initiates an oral history project to honor veterans in the community. The veterans chosen to be interviewed are likely to be members of the community, and the questions asked will be those of particular interest to the community. For example, a community defined by addiction treatment, may emphasize veterans' stories around addiction management. This kind of a project usually consists of multiple oral histories of community veterans with the intention to preserve interviews in a library and to create a lot of public outreach.

While oral history is collaborative work, oral historians focus more on the "care for the veteran" like building trust, establishing rapport, honoring reciprocity and protecting privacy. Ensure you maintain the collaborative spirit throughout the project. Tips:

- Conduct regular meetings
- Communicate with all stakeholders
- Treat everyone like partners
- Ensuring all participants feel valued
- Ensure transparency about decision-making and finances
- Respond to feedback
- Listen with empathy and care
- Donate energy and space to public programming, if applicable, for public dialogue and community engagement with question-and-answer segments, food and drink (for more welcoming atmosphere)

Oral History Project to Create Research Document

The veteran experience always has and always will be the subject of research, as we all attempt to understand the experience of war. Whether interviews are conducted by journalists researching for a book or high school students writing a term paper, or professional oral historians, the experience of identifying a veteran narrator, developing rapport, and listening carefully to their stories requires a deep knowledge of oral history best practices. In this type of project, interviews are intended to be used by researchers in the present and far into the future. They will likely be deposited in a research repository – a large library or digital archive – available to a broad audience. Interviewers are usually subject experts, interview questions are directed toward personal memories of broad historical events, and archiving is carefully done.

Here is a short questionnaire to guide your thinking. As you consider each question, please consider the ideal timeframe for your project. Do you envision a long-term, ongoing project or simpler, short-term project?

Oral History Project Brainstorming Questions

1. What do you want the project to accomplish?
2. What categories of people do you want to interview?
3. What kinds of information do you wish get from the interviews?
4. How should interviews be recorded: Audio? Video? Both? Distance or in person?
5. What kind of access do you wish for the interviews?
6. How do you envision the interviews to be used?
7. How will the program be funded? Funding ideas?
8. Personnel: Who will do the interviews? Transcribing? Cataloging? Preservation? In house or outsource? What will be the permanent home for the interviews?
9. Where will final oral histories be kept? Will they be available online? What kinds of access do you wish for them to have?

Setting Goals and Objectives With the Veteran Community

As you contemplate the project needs, consider the needs of the veteran and/or veteran participants or organization. Include them in your planning and give them a strong voice in the conversation. This will create a win-win situation for the overall objectives and goals of the project. In an ideal environment, veterans oral history projects will be what Mindy Thompson Fulliove, calls an "empowered collaboration." By this she means partaking in a strategy in which at the start, the planners/organizers will conduct a detailed assessment of the needs and interests of the environment/culture/community and from that assessment create a list of priorities that will help guide the next steps. The implementation (conducting and processing oral histories) and assessment. Community members, whether war veterans, family members, or support community will be your greatest assets in keeping the project on track. Whether you are conducting a private family interview or working within a community for a more formal project, it is imperative to establish a rapport with the veteran, thereby inviting and encouraging them to be more comfortable with you during the process (516–523). Also, planning your project includes knowing exactly what you want to accomplish and why. Assess your own interests in both oral history and in veterans' stories to determine if an oral history project or just an informal interview is the best approach for achieving your goals.

Designing and Planning Your Veterans Oral History Project

A note about planning, timelines, and the human factor: Though it is easy to estimate the time schedule for steps like conducting an interview, traveling to the interview and transcription, it is very difficult to estimate the amount of time it might take to identify potential narrators, meet them at a place where they are comfortable, and to build their trust. This can take days, months, or years. But gaining this trust is an essential ingredient for your success, so it is worthwhile. When planning your project timeline, be sure to factor in extra time required to build trust with veterans. Whatever your project design is, calculate a realistic timeline to include all steps in the process, including the extra time involved in gaining the trust of the veterans. Be sure to build in some flexibility for situations you cannot control, such as waiting for the veterans to be ready to talk. Circumstances will determine how time-consuming and involved you will need to be in order to accomplish your goals.

Planning Decisions Include

- Whom you wish to interview (specific names or particular qualities of chosen narrators)
- Partnerships and collaborations
- A projected timeline for a completed project
- Interview method(s) (see Chapter 11: Interviewing War Veterans)
- Scope of project (the number of interviews you hope to conduct)
- Topics to be discussed during the interview
- Other activities that will be in your project
- The final product of your project
- The projected ways the oral history interviews will be used
- Who will have access to these materials, and
- What will happen to the interviews

When considering how to plan and manage a veterans oral history project, Barbara Sommer's *Planning a Community Oral History Project* Volume 2 (in the *Community Oral History Toolkit*) is an excellent source. She focuses specifically on the initial steps in getting started, project design, planning for people and infrastructure, equipment and planning, and finding funding sources for the project. Sommer provides an excellent resource for those new and old to practicing oral history.

Sometimes the planning and managing stages may be started by one person but may expand as the project develops. Sommer stresses the importance and care taken during the initial planning stages that can apply to most oral history projects. It is during the initial phrases of the project that planners have the opportunity to discuss design, team members, equipment, and funding. Sommer also shares valuable information about project funding and funding sources. It is imperative to have early conversations about funding regardless of the type of veterans oral history project, whether it is personal, private, family, community, etc. Since technology quickly advances, making early decisions about the types of equipment needed will prove fundamentally important for the overall quality production of the interviews (see Chapter 9).

That said, unforeseen circumstances may arise that require you to rethink the project and that is just fine. Interviewees may mention other veterans who would be likely candidates for interviews. New topics or new approaches to existing topics may arise during the course of interviews that prompts you to go in a different direction. And there are also practical factors that arise. Perhaps an interviewee backs out, gets sick or goes on an extended vacation. Or, since the pandemic has forced many of us to stay distant, it may be that you switch to an online interview format. In other words, it important to stay flexible as you move through the project.

While veterans oral history is collaborative work, oral historians focus more on the "care for the veteran" like building trust, establishing rapport, honoring reciprocity, and protecting privacy between veteran and interviewer. Pay attention to how to maintain the collaborative spirit as the project develops. These steps require good communication with everyone involved in planning and implementation and remember to be transparent about decision-making and finances. Treat all team members like partners, make sure all feel valued and heard. Hold regular meetings, be responsive and adaptive to feedback, listen with empathy and care, donate energy and space to public programming, if applicable, for public dialogue and community engagement with question-and-answer segments, food, and drink (for more welcoming atmosphere).

An oral history project team should seek answers to conceptual problems; it should ask difficult questions that challenge cozy assumptions about community, such as: how do individuals (and communities) tell stories that make sense of their lives? What is the relationship between personal narrative and identity? What can we learn from the analysis of the language and from of the patterns of speech and of silence? How do narrators both draw upon and create cultural genres of storytelling" (Perks and Thomson 214). Sady Sullivan also comments that "community-based learning involves encouraging participants to historicize their understandings of [mixed heritage] identity and culture and engage in [racial justice] dialogue" (254).

A veterans oral history project can arise in a number of ways. Sometimes it arises because of a moment, such as a culminating project for a community's veterans memorial. Sometimes it comes from a higher agency, perhaps a city or county veterans group, that needs more information about their local veterans in order to better serve them. Sometimes it is a graduate student or journalist who is seeking the untold human story of veterans integration into community life after combat. Or maybe it happens around the dining room table, when three generations of a family want to hear grandpa's full war story.

From whatever the origin, designing an oral history project involves a number of steps. As an oral historian, consider conducting a detailed assessment of the community, create a list of priorities and resources to guide your plan and project, communicate and connect with the veteran community often, paying careful attention to the emotional needs of the veteran. Balance the design for your veterans oral history project between your intended goals and the needs of the veteran community. Include all interested parties: you as project manager, the veteran(s), community partners, funding agencies, and any other resource personnel. It usually takes several planning meetings to figure out goals, objectives, outcomes/final products, funding allocations, guidelines, and procedures.

There are several approaches for structuring veterans oral history projects, from designing the project in phrases, by the calendar year, or by goals accomplished. Be sure you understand what is important to the veteran participants. Goals and objectives will emerge and ultimately evolve during the time of trust-building with the veterans. As you spend time with the community of veterans, you will begin to understand their very specific needs and how your time interviewing and documenting their experiences may help them meet those needs, resolve issues, build a support system or tell their stories. Be sure to revise your plan and incorporate the suggestions of the veterans into your stated goals and objectives. If you are just beginning to plan, you can actually plan engage the help of your veteran/community and/or community partners. Give your veteran community a clear voice and vision in the project. This may encourage participation and motivate them to share their stories.

Even if your goals and objectives shift throughout the course of your project, addressing them at the onset is an essential first step and will create a roadmap for the implementation of your project.

When and How to Include Veterans in the Project Design

Veterans, themselves, are at the heart of any oral history project, and they can serve in a number of roles, not just as the interviewee. One good way to incorporate veterans is to develop an advisory group for the project that includes mostly veterans. This group will feel engaged in the project and can contribute solid concrete ideas to the design, as to what questions to ask and how to ask questions gently. They can be ambassadors for the project, simply by being a part of the advisory group. Their presence can build trust within the community. In some projects, veterans can engage in practical tasks such as interviewing, transcribing, doing historical research, and participating in public events. Ways in which you can get other veterans involved is visiting and attending local veterans organizations and programs, becoming familiar with veterans who are instrumental in activities that attract others, setting up meetings to discuss how you can get involved and how your project may align with their current programs and meetings.

Project Team

Whether you are an individual planning to interview family members who are veterans or you are administering a large-scale grant, your project requires multiple areas of expertise. In small projects such as family interviews, the team may consist of one person performing all functions. In a larger oral history program or archives, a project team is usually formed to include the expertise needed. These tasks may be distributed among specialists, with a project manager to coordinate all their efforts.

- **Project management** – the person in this position coordinates all the efforts of the project from the very beginning to the very end, to include initial planning, keeping records, training staff and volunteering, coordinating interview steps, overseeing transfer to the archives, and coordinating public events and outreach at the end of the project.
- **Interviewing** – the person in this position will conduct preliminary research, help prepare questions, make initial contact with veterans prior to the interview, assist with completing any consent forms, and interview each veteran.
- **Transcribing** – the person in this position will be responsible for all issues related to transcribing recorded interviews as well as doing the actual transcriptions.
- **Subject expertise** – the person in this position will work closely with the project manager and interviewer to conduct research about each war and the veteran and on the topics of the specific interviews to prepare interview questions and prepare for the interviewing sessions.
- **Technical expertise** – the person in this position or team of people will assist with selecting the proper equipment, updating the equipment due to technological advances and help educate and train others about the use of the equipment and for selecting and operating equipment, creating a protocol for digital formats for capture and storage.
- **Archiving plan** – the person in this position will work with the project management on archival plans for the transcribed and digital materials.
- **Community outreach** – the person in this position will be responsible for establishing relationships with community partnerships who can support and/ or assist in the overall project.

Expenses for Your Project

Money plays a role, usually but not always, a limiting role in the design and execution of any project. Fortunately, in veterans oral history the balance sheet can vary enormously and you can have a successful project that is low budget or high budget. Researching funding sources should be an early phase of your project design plan. Almost all expenses concern people or technology, and both of these categories can be available at little or no cost, in exchange for human or in-kind services. For example, a successful family oral history project could take place at no cost at all if family members follow the instructions in this book for project design, interview technique, and they use recording equipment they already own to carefully audio- or video-record interviews and preserve them. At the other extreme would be a research project for a large library or a book. This project might include expenses for travel to interviews, high-quality recording equipment, research, and transcription. Both projects could be successful for their goals.

Securing Funding Your Project

When you are planning a project, consider the expenses for conducting the project and how you will meet those expenses. Funding sources for veterans oral history projects can depend on the type of interviewing or project as well as the type of final product you will produce. You can seek funding through partnerships with museums, historical societies, local arts, and humanities organizations. Local community organizations and businesses are great sources for funding for community oral history projects. Federal, state, and local governmental agencies may offer competitive grants focusing on veterans oral history such as humanities council, historical societies, and the National Endowment for Humanities. The overall project goals, the number of veterans to be interviewed, and project design of your proposed oral history project may depend somewhat on funding, so it is always a good idea to have a several funding options when you begin to plan the project. Your funding checklist may include some or all of the following:

*   (computer and recording) equipment
*   travel costs
*   transcription fees
*   (space) rental fees
*   supplies/resources

Community Involvement

Get the community or other veterans involved in your project. This step fits very well with your trust-building activities and experiences with your veteran/community (see Chapter 6). If you have established a good rapport with them, then they will help you build support for your work. They can spread the word to other veterans about your project and programming and begin to build momentum for others to participate in the interviewing process. Once the first few veterans participate in their interviews, they will understand what is involved and can explain it to others. Building and maintaining their trust from the beginning is essential to building strong support among other veterans. Community involvement may take additional work. Consider inviting community members to participate in your project by hosting or sponsoring events where veterans can share their experiences with the project. Community support may also come from press releases, social media posts, public announcements, and word of mouth.

Publicizing Your Project

Determining project expenses may also involve soliciting support and will depend on a few variables. You must be willing to meet with different people and organizations to discuss your project and how their specific organization may be able to best support your work. You can solicit support for your own veterans oral history project through press releases in your local newspaper and social media posts, posting flyers in local organizations and surrounding communities, word of mouth, etc. If you are seeking specific support from particular organizations, schedule a meeting so you can talk with them personally about your project, its goals and objectives and how they may be able to support your work.

Keeping Records

Keeping accurate, up-to-date records is essential to good oral history practice. You can use and/or adapt the forms below (samples are in Appendices).

- Interview Questionnaire
- Biographical data sheet
- Interviewer's Release/Consent Form
- Veteran's Release/Consent Form
- Photograph Log

Questions for Veterans Oral History Projects

This section include examples of existing veterans oral history projects that greatly influenced my own work. Visiting with other oral historians, community scholars, and documentarians who have worked with military and war veterans to see how their works and projects emerged was a high point of my research. Here are some questions that focused our discussions:

1. Describe your oral history project and/or collection. Be as specific as possible.
2. Did you make a distinction between military veterans and combat veterans? Why or why not?
3. Describe your thought process in designing your project? Was it community-based? Institutional-based? Personal/family project?
4. What were your funding sources? Did they match your budget needs?
5. Describe the size of your project team, and the roles of each member?
6. How did you train and/or prepare them?

7. How important was it that your team/group be familiar with working with veterans and any special issues that could arise during the project?
8. What were the initial goals of your project? Did they change over time? If so, how and why?
9. How many oral histories did you plan to collect? Did you accomplish that goal?
10. Describe the step-by-step methodology you used to collect the oral histories.
11. How did you recruit? Invite? Select? veteran participants for your project?
12. After the veterans agreed to participate in your project, how did you keep them interested over time?
13. How involved were you personally in the project? What were your specific roles?
14. Approximately, how long did each interviews last (what was the duration of the interview)?
15. Where did the interviews take place? Were they conducted in person or remotely?
16. Did you use audio or video recording or both?
17. How were the interviews processed? Were they transcribed? Indexed? Archived? Preserved?
18. What other ways were they interviews used beyond your project?
19. Did the veterans share other items with you, such as photographs or artifacts? If so, what type of items were shared and how were they used during the process or the project?
20. Did any special circumstances occur during the interviews that created any concern for the interviewer? Did the interviewer ever feel "out of control," of "out of her league of expertise"? If so, how was this handled?
21. When the project ended, did you keep up contact with the veteran participants? describe
22. What additional resources were required for you to complete the project?
23. Did you have a timeline for the overall project? Were you able to follow your projected timeline?
24. Is there anything you would have done differently? Explain.

Examples of Existing Veterans Oral History

Thirty Days with My Father: Finding Peace from Wartime PTSD

A veterans oral history project that was conducted to interview a family member, specifically a child (daughter) interviewing a parent (father) is Christal Presley's *Thirty Days with My Father: Finding Peace from Wartime PTSD*. It tells a story of a daughter afraid to return to her childhood home that was engulfed by the trauma of war. Her story was told through oral history interviews, conversations and journaling. Her main objective was to "talk and listen to her father every day for thirty days in a row [to] portray this remote and secret world of America's rural traumatized veterans and their families suffering in silence and confusion." Besides focusing on the trauma of war, her veterans oral history project also focused on diverse issues of gender, geography, and family.

Through these conversations, father and daughter were about to unpack his legacy of war intertwined with war trauma. The use of oral history in her memoir perhaps was not by design or planning, but that methodology makes it more poignant for her audience. She approached this project organically in a search for her own healing from a painful past. In 2009, Presley's intent was to talk to her father for thirty days in hopes of dealing with issues from her childhood. "Her memoir gives not only a detailed account of the ripple effects of PTSD on children, but also an inside look at the recovery of a father and grown daughter."

Presley's father, Delmer Presley, returned home from his service in Vietnam dealing with flashbacks, nightmares, and suicidal thoughts. She considered him an unpredictable father. She discusses how her childhood memories were intertwined with his behavior. After not speaking to her father regularly for thirteen years, she attended a writing workshop and the speaker asked, "what if you wrote about the thing you fear the most?" She decided on doing a thirty-day therapeutic conversation with her father. After her own reluctance to start the project and her father's retraction of his willingness to participate, she continued to ask him anyway: "'you're still doing the project with me, aren't you?' I ask when my dad picks up the phone. Knowing how difficult this is going to be suddenly feels overwhelming. "It'll just be asking some questions, Dad," I say. "'Questions about what?'" he wants to know. He sounds suspicious. [He responded] "Questions about the war. About Vietnam. I don't want to talk about the war," he snaps. "I don't know anything about a war." [She thought] I feel as if I've just been slapped in the face. Even though I had initially hoped – and assumed – that he'd refuse to talk to me, when he'd said yes, I got my hopes up. Now they are dashed again, and I am flooded with memories of all the sudden, unexplained mood swings he had when I was growing up and of how frightening they were to me. All I can do is hang up the phone."

Throughout her conversations, Presley soon realized how much she and her father had in common, other than experiencing the symptoms of PTSD. Her father admitted that playing his guitar was therapy for him just as she used writing as her therapy. In the book foreword, Edward Tick writes, "we are reminded once again – when one person goes to war, nobody in that person's circle escapes wounding, either during service or after." Presley uses the oral history methodology to explore how war affects children and to illustrate what some call intergenerational PTSD or secondary traumatization. Her question-and-answer format was conversational in an attempt to put her father at ease, his PTSD and her own lifetime of trauma. From thirty days of interviews, each conversation was given its own chapter within the book, and each chapter concludes with a journal entry of her childhood memories. The design of the memoir reflects a bit of fragmentation that one may often feel when living with PTSD. Presley's conversations and interviews with her father are directly related to those childhood memories that she shares through her journal. She was able to ask her father about being drafted into the war, the Tet Offensive, Agent Orange, counseling, and many other difficult topics. Her project evolved from a personal desire to heal from a life of trauma that was rooted in her father's service in the Vietnam War. Since she focused her project and book on PTSD and the psychological trauma of war, it was popular in the healthcare field because it speaks directly to how to better understand and, if needed, provide treat for our current returning veterans.

A Thousand Words: Photographs by Vietnam Veterans

I also include as a case study Martin Tucker's *A Thousand Words: Photographs by Vietnam Veterans* because this is an example of a veteran practicing oral history with other veterans. He is a Vietnam-era US Navy veteran, an award-winning photojournalist, author, and filmmaker. After completing the oral history and exhibit, he retained the publishing rights to the project and published a book about the work, *Vietnam Photographs From North Carolina Veterans – The Memories They Brought Home*. In 2004, when Martin Tucker was serving as the director of photography at the Sawtooth School for Visual Art in Winston-Salem, North Carolina, he had an idea to borrow local Vietnam Veteran's negatives from their tours so his students could print the veteran's images in a darkroom class. He posted flyers around the Triad area that simply said, "Seeking Vietnam Veterans" and his request for negatives. Veterans began to call but instead of negatives they offered their personal photos and Kodachrome slides. As numerous veterans and boxes of images kept coming, he formed a committee of volunteers to expand the project into an exhibit. Since he only had $70 in his department account, everyone solicited funds from businesses and the community. That framed exhibit of sixty images, titled "A Thousand Words: Photographs by Vietnam Veterans," opened in Winston-Salem and traveled nationwide for thirteen years. After the exhibit was displayed for a year at the North Carolina Museum of History and, at their request, Martin donated the exhibit to the museum. It is now in their permanent collection and a second version will continue to travel state-wide. Tucker's oral history project illustrates how they often start very organically with very little preparation, money or intention but once started, it gained momentum rapidly and he had to go backward in a sense to cover consent and use of property. In 2005, Tucker said:

> As I look around my office at the Sawtooth School for Visual Art, I find it hard to believe that not too long ago I was surrounded by boxes of photographs. Not just a few boxes, but boxes stacked from the floor to the ceiling. 4,000 photographs, to be exact. All the result of a flyer that simply said Seeking Vietnam Veterans. It had started out as an idea to give my black & white photography students something different to print in the darkroom. Post a few flyers around the Triad asking Vietnam veterans to loan us any black & white negatives they might still have from their tours and my students would make enlargements from them. We'd give the veterans a nice print for participating, tack the photos on the bulletin board and hopefully the students would get a history lesson in the bargain. And that would be the end of it.
>
> *(Firesheets)*

As a Vietnam-era veteran, Martin decided to call the local veterans organizations and asked if he could come in and make a short pitch. He informed them, "If you have any negatives and could loan them to us, I promise we'll take good care of them. You can even come over and watch your photograph come up in the developing tray." The posters and the meetings help spread the word and a few weeks later the phone started to ring. The veterans told Martin that they didn't have any negatives but they had photographs, small 3 × 5″ color and black and white photographs, Kodachrome slides, and photographs that had been in closets and under beds for thirty years which they were mostly faded, torn, and dusty that had been pushed deep into the darkness and out of sight. When Martin started scheduling appointment times, he began to consider if maybe this was more than just a class project.

The first veteran who offered Martin a photograph was a friend, a businessman, and an avid photographer, who had also taken Martin's class. When Martin mentioned the Vietnam idea to him, he simply said he had a few photographs, and Martin did not even know that he was a Vietnam Veteran. Later in the process, this friend's opinion became very important as photographs began to flood in. The second veteran to come in did not bring in photographs but had an overwhelming curiosity and concern about why Martin wanted all these pictures. He was a past-president of the local chapter of the Vietnam Veterans of America, so Martin assured him that he was doing this for the right reasons, because he was a Vietnam-era veteran himself and his intentions were honorable. This same veteran, after talking to Martin, came back three weeks later with five prized photographs and a story of being pinned down in a firefight the first week he was in Vietnam. Martin was not yet prepared for the stories that would be attached to these photographs, something not unusual when working with war veterans. Oral history projects like this one often begin organically. Martin soon realized that he needed to keep a journal of his meetings with the veterans because they did not want to just drop off the photos, they also wanted to talk. They shared very emotional stories with him. Years later, these photographs triggered both memories and strong feelings. Even though some of the details were a little fuzzy, they still remembered names and dates.

All the veterans Martin talked to about the project knew someone who had served in Vietnam. Martin began to connect the dots from one veteran to another. As the veterans became more interested and photos kept coming, Martin decided to form a committee and put up a formal exhibit of the photographs. He began soliciting for donations to cover the cost of ink, paper and frames. Sawtooth students and volunteers from local middle schools, high schools, colleges, and the community came in to digitally repair the old photographs before they printed enlargements. The number one rule was to maintain the integrity of the original photograph. After he had secured a location for the exhibit, framed it, and was making plans for a reception, a committee member who was a commentator for the local NPR station made a suggestion that forever changed the exhibit. "Why not invite the vets back, let them look at the photos we chose for the exhibit and tape-record their thoughts and comments on their photos?" So, on a Sunday afternoon in May, the quiet, mild-mannered, and middle-aged men came back one at a time and remembered. And wept. And began to find closure. Their moving comments during the viewing became the quotes that now hang below every photograph. Martin received calls from veterans in Virginia, South Carolina, Florida and as far away as Washington State. They all had photos and just wanted to make sure that the story was told fairly and accurately.

Martin wondered: How do you take 4,000 photographs and tell a soldier's story of what it was like to serve in Vietnam? The key to that question is a soldier's story. This exhibit and project were not intended to be a story of whether we should have been in Vietnam. It was always about the soldiers in Vietnam – about what the soldier's saw in Vietnam. They only had room for sixty framed 8 × 10 photographs in that first exhibit, so whenever Martin got stumped on whether to keep a photo in or not, he asked myself a simple question: "would a Vietnam vet be able to stand in front of that photograph and say, "that's exactly the way it was, right there." If it passed that test, it stayed in. The majority of the vets who participated had never spoken about their experiences in Vietnam. Not to their parents, not to their wives and not to their children. They didn't come home to a parade. Wives have told me, "we just don't talk about it." For the first time, those vets have been able to stand in front of those photographs with their children, parents and spouses and say proudly, "that's the way it was. I just never could say it, but those photographs say it for me."

After that first exhibit, it began a nation-wide tour. It was viewed by over 20,000 people at the Air Zoo Museum in Kalamazoo, Michigan. 1,000 people saw it in the first week in small-town Waynesville, North Carolina. The Comment Book that goes with it is full of personal reflections about brothers, fathers, sons, uncles, and friends who served and never spoke of it. Some lost limbs, some lost their innocence while others lost their lives. The veterans write their military branch, company names, numbers, and dates of service. Family members say, "I just want to see what they went through." The communities say, "thanks for remembering." The exhibit is an iconic piece that nobody's ever thought to put together because it comes from the veterans themselves. The photographs in the exhibit are not from professional (photo)journalists. They came from little cameras those guys had in their backpacks or that hung from strings around their necks, and they mailed the film home to be developed" (Firesheets).

The Natick Veterans Oral History Project

The Natick Veterans Oral History Project at the Morse Institute Library in Natick, Massachusetts started in 1998 as a result of Eugene Dugdale, a World War II veteran and only Pearl Harbor survivor from Natick, approaching the library about his concerns of World War II veterans dying without having told their stories. The Natick Veterans Oral History Project began by working with several organizations, like local veterans organizations, the Natick Public Schools, and Natick Pegasus (the local cable access station). The project is supported by both private and public funding, including ongoing support from the Commonwealth of Massachusetts, and is designed specifically for Massachusetts veterans who served in the Armed Forces, of any country not just the United States, as well as for those who helped during World War II on the home front in areas such as border or light patroller and factory workers. The veteran can either be interviewed in a private setting at the Morse Library, in the veteran's home or another designated site. Once the interviews are completed, they are copied to DVDs, that are archived at the library, cataloged in the library, and made available for public use and also given to the veteran for personal history and private use. Both video and audio versions of the veteran interviews are posted on the project's website and made available for download. In 2019, the Natick Veterans Oral History Project had 340 interviews available on DVD and has expanded its collection, through state-funded grants, for books, DVDs, and CDs on related subjects that focus on wartime and home front experiences, regional histories, New England and Massachusetts participation in wartime efforts as well as historical wartime reference materials. All interviews are videorecorded and available in the library for checkout to community members.

Bibliography

Firesheets, Tina. "Former Photojournalist Martin Tucker to Release Book of Photos Taken by N.C. Vietnam Veterans." *News & Record*, August 11, 2009. https://greensboro.com/entertainment/former-photojournalist-martin-tucker-to-release-book-of-photos-taken-by-n-c-vietnam-veterans/article_34695388–8971–5c9a-bbc4-bc2d33294c66.html. Accessed November 16, 2021. York: Rowman & Littlefield Publishers, Inc., 2012.

Fulliove, Mindy Thompson. "Psychiatric Implications of Displacement: Contributions from Psychology of Place." *The American Journal of Psychiatry* vol. 153, 1996, pp. 516–523.

Natick Veterans Oral History Project. https://natickveterans.com. Accessed November 16, 2021.

Presley, Christal. *Thirty Days with My Father: Finding Peace with Wartime PTSD*. Florida: Health Communications, Inc., 2012.

Robert Perks and Alistair Thomson. *The Oral History Reader*. New York, Routledge, 1998.

Sommer, Barbara. "Managing a Community Oral History Project Volume 3." *Community Oral History Toolkit*, edited by Nancy MacKay, Mary Kay Quinlan, Barbara W. Sommer. California: Left Coast Press, 2013.

Sommer, Barbara. "Planning a Community Oral History Project Volume 2." *Community Oral History Toolkit*, edited by Nancy MacKay, Mary Kay Quinlan, Barbara W. Sommer. California: Left Coast Press, 2013.

Sullivan, Sadie. "Public Homeplaces: Collaboration and Care in Oral History Project Design." *Beyond Women's Words: Feminisms and The Practices of Oral History in the Twenty-first Century*, edited by Katrina Srigley, Stacey Zembrzycki and Franca Icaovetta. New York: Routledge, 2018, pp. 236–243.

Tucker, Martin. *Vietnam Photographs From North Carolina: The Memories They Brought Home*. Charleston: The History Press, 2019.

9

RECORDING TECHNIQUES

The Oral History Association's Principles and Best Practices state, "interviewers should create, when possible, a high-quality recording of the interview (audio or video format) to capture the narrator's interview accurately with consideration of future audiences and long-term preservation." This broad statement provides a foundation for filling in the blanks to develop a recording plan for your project that meets your recording needs within the human, budget, and technology parameters.

All oral history best practices recommend recording in digital formats and instructions here will follow the digital only protocols. In a digital environment, the interview you record becomes a digital file with a life of its own. The digital file can be easily transferred to a family member's listening device (sound or video), to an archive, or to the Internet. It can be edited, preserved, shared, restricted or any of the other behaviors the file will require during its life. Whether you are recording an interview for your own family, for future generations, or for an international archive, a digital file has the best chance for getting into the hands and eyes of its intended audience.

Existing Equipment

In many cases, equipment you already own – such as computers, mobile devices, smartphones, and tablets – may be used for audio recording and video recording. With the rapid advancements and ever-evolving technology, those involved in military and veterans oral history must first ask themselves, "how will the oral history interviews be used?" The answer to this question will allow you to make sound decisions about what specific technology to purchase and use early in your process, whether the interview should be conducted as an in-person interview or as a distance interview as well as determining budgeting and funding sources.

According to the Oral History Centre at the University of Winnipeg, there are pros and cons to recording with a mobile device/smartphone; however, the

DOI: 10.4324/9781003280323-12

decision to use one over a stand abalone recorder will always depend on how you plan to use the oral history interviews. Using a mobile device keeps you from having to purchase a recorder. If you need an external microphone then there are affordable compact options that will complement your device. If you are planning to use the collected oral history interviews for a more personal or private reason opposed to donating them to a repository or database, then using a mobile device/ smart phone should not present many challenges. However, if using a mobile device/smart phone is your only option for recording interviews for a more public or funded project, then you should be aware of some possible challenges:

- Built-in microphones may not be as good as the ones on standalone recorders
- Managing some of the hardware controls and monitoring on the mobile device during the interview
- Potential for recording to fail
- Limited storage on mobile device/smart phone due to file sharing
- May not be able to easily change memory card on mobile device/smart phone
- Transfer of files may not be as simple as on a stand-alone recorder

If you decide to use a mobile device/smart phone then familiarize yourself with the device before the recording session. Based on how your oral history interviews will be used, make sure that your device has enough memory/storage and power (battery life); that notifications are muted and will not interrupt recoding; that applications are updated to best support the recording; that you can properly handle the device during the interview to ensure stability; and that the device can support the transferability of the files. In order to get the highest quality interview possible, you should always test the technology in different settings to make sure it works for you before you attempt the recording with your mobile device/smart phone.

For computer recording, you can use:

- USB microphones, which plug directly into a computer's USB port; and
- low-cost or free recording programs

For smartphones and tablets, you can use:

- attachable microphones; and
- recording apps or web-based audio sharing services that might be helpful for voice recordings

Audio Versus Video

One of the first decisions in planning your project is whether to record interviews using audio, video and/or both. There are benefits and disadvantages of both and the choice depends on the goals of your project and the wishes of the narrator, the budget, the equipment available, and whether your oral history is for a private family collection, personal research, community archive, or institutional collection.

Audio

The primary advantage of audio recording is that it is easier, less expensive, and the technology is simpler, so audio-only interviews can typically be conducted by one person at a relatively low cost. The disadvantage is that the visual information and nuances that video recording captures will be lost. An alternative to capturing visual images on video is to take photographs of veterans and other artifacts that they may share. If you decide to conduct audio interviews, select recording equipment that the interviewer can easily master and use effectively. Practice using the microphone in a space similar or the same as your interviewing environment, listening for outside sounds such as an air-conditioning unit, dripping faucets, noisy plumbing, audible voices from family members and children, pets, and noisy appliances.

Video

Video recording is more complicated at every level, from choosing appropriate camera equipment, to setting up the equipment properly to fixing issues if the equipment malfunctions. Video recording can be more expensive and more complicated technically. From a preservation point of view, video uses much more storage and depending on the staging setup, it can involve studio space, lighting, videographer, etc. You may purchase your own video recording equipment, borrow video equipment from an institution or hire a videographer for your project. If you intend to use the equipment for future projects, purchasing your own equipment may be less expensive than hiring a videographer. Also, with video recordings, you may also have to purchase lighting equipment (if recording inside a studio), so you will have the best possible environment and setting for the actual interview. "A Brief Guide to Basic Technology Planning for Oral History Projects" suggests that you conduct a test run with your equipment with another person before the first interview. During this practice run, please consider the following questions.

1. How is the lighting? Do you need special lighting equipment?
2. What placement of the microphone produces the best audio? If it's a clip-on mic, figure out how you are going to get it on your interviewee without making them uncomfortable.
3. Where will your interviewee be in the frame of your video? What looks the best? Keep in mind that your interviewee may shift in his/her chair, and if you don't have a designated camera operator, they may move out of the frame. Will the interviewer be filmed? If so, do you need an additional camera?
4. What location will you film in? The interviewee's home? The oral history office? A formal film studio? There are pros and cons for each choice, for example, filming in the interviewee's home

5. How will you handle interruptions?
6. Depending on your recording media, how will you know to switch the tape/ SD card (in specific cameras or digital devices)? (Mann)

Nancy MacKay in *Curating Oral Histories: From Interview to Archive* provides some pros and cons that might help you decide between recording in audio or video. Please see Table 1 below:

TABLE 1 Audio Versus Video Pros and Cons

Audio	*Video*
Highlight voice quality	Provides richer portrait of narrator through facial expression, clothing, and setting
Narrator may prefer not to appear on video	Can film supplementary information
Recoding setting requires only a quiet space	Recording setting requires attention to lighting and background as well as acoustics
Space can be informal, where narrator might be more comfortable	Studio setting is often preferred
Audio interviews are recorded in uncompressed formats	Most digital video is compressed. The best practice is to record interviews in professional quality formats
Recording technology simpler and often less expensive. Household devices can provide good recording.	Recording equipment more complicated and costly. Can involve multiple cameras and lights
Little training needed	Multiple issues streaming on the Internet

When making the final decisions between whether to use audio or video, MacKay contends that while audio technology can be simpler and less expensive, it does place more emphasis on voice and there are standards and best practices in place. With video recording, while technology might be a more expensive and a bit more complicated due to large file sizes, it can provide a richer and more engaging picture of the veteran (93).

Microphones. An external microphone is generally recommended over built-in microphone to better control sound quality. Use one or two microphones depending on the number of participants, I recommend a handheld condenser microphone with a directional pickup pattern.

Selecting the Proper Equipment

Selecting the proper equipment will be determined by a number of factors, such as the purpose of your oral history project, the cost of the project, and how the oral history collection will be used. As mentioned earlier this, book deals only with digital audio or video recording equipment, which has become the standard for all oral history interviews. It is easier to operate and, in most cases, more affordable.

When selecting equipment, remember to consider devices that adequately record and preserve high quality sound. Depending on the goals and objectives of your project, other considerations for equipment might include batteries, electrical extension cords, microphones, lighting, and/or computers.

Digital and video recorders store audio files on digital media like memory cards, allowing files to be transferred to a computer for processing. Digital recording is the modern standard and allows for the highest quality and integrity of audio files. We recommend recorders that feature:

- XLR inputs, which accommodate a wider variety of microphones;
- capacity to record WAV (also called PCM) audio files;
- removable media, like Compact Flash or SD cards
- Microphone accessories, such as stands, mounts, or cables may be useful as well.
- Use headphones to monitor sound from the recorder. We recommend over-the-ear, closed-back-style headphones to block out background noise.

Distance-Interviewing With Veterans

In early 2020, oral historians were faced with an enormous challenge: how does one continue documenting and recording veterans oral history during a global health pandemic? In the early months of the COVID-19 pandemic, we were probably not giving much thought to our scholarship and fieldwork as concerns about our health and public safety were the main priority. But as the weeks turned into months in lockdown, those of us in the middle of veterans oral history projects had to take a long pause and re-consider how, or even if, to proceed. The very thought of conducting either a telephone interview or an online video interview during this time presented a new set of challenges, from audio quality, selecting a video recording platform to properly preparing the veteran for the recording session without being in the same location.

If you will record with a smartphone, the computer or even via telephone; the background distractions that might be present in the environments of both the interviewer and the veteran, such as children and pets; and varying your questionnaires. All of these possible challenges should be thoroughly considered for distancing interviews. In 2019, I began working on a new veterans oral history project for the North Carolina African American Veterans Lineage Day (AAVLD). Well into the project and after the preliminary interviews had been conducted, the world shut down in 2020 due to the pandemic. My documentary team and community partners, along with our funding agency, had to reconsider the entire project and how it needed to change quickly to stay focused on the project goals. Funded projects, especially those supported by grant monies, often have deadlines and project outcomes and deliverables. Face-to-face interviews and community events to share stories were immediately cancelled as we tried to figure out what to do next, if anything, during this time. In-person meetings with community partners moved to emails, phone calls and TEAMS and ZOOM meetings. The pandemic halted our ability to travel to the homes of our veteran participants or even public spaces to record the interviews, work collaboratively in designated spaces to prepare and process the collected materials, and meet in community settings to share the collected stories with others. Since our veteran community was World War II veterans already in their nineties, we had to be pay extra attention to health concerns and time sensitivity due to their age. It was almost impossible to conduct any follow-up or additional interviews to complete what we began in 2019. It was also quite difficult to quickly transition into the digital realm for this purpose.

As a team, we made some tough but necessary decisions to use the interview footage that we had already collected and to seek permission from the funding agency to keep our timeline and change some of deliverables of the project. With permission granted and not knowing the changing circumstances due to the pandemic, we altered the final products for the project from a series of films that would cover African Americans who served in various wars to a dedicated feature documentary film that focused on the World War II veterans we initially met and interviewed as well as several other digitally produced items. Unfortunately, some of the veterans who were featured in the documentary film died during our postproduction process and did not get the opportunity to see the completed project.

The pandemic raised a number of challenges for those oral historians working with vulnerable populations and those with health concerns. The project team had to be mindful of the overall demographics of the veterans being interviewed, such as age, location, health, comfortability, willingness to continue to participate, environment, and exposure. Even in our consideration to try to get more video or audio footage during the pandemic, we were uncertain of the veteran's access to and ability to use technology. Due to these various uncertainties caused by the pandemic, our project team made sure the deliverables from the project were available in a digital format and available via the Internet. We relied heavily on photography and digital platforms to share the collected stories with various communities. The changes to the project satisfied both the funding agency and the veteran participants.

The British Oral History Society created an advice guide on remote oral history interviewing during the COVID-19 pandemic. But most importantly, the guide raised questions that should be considered when deciding to conduct oral history interviews in-person during the pandemic, especially if it might endanger the health of the interviewers, the interviewee, and all others involved. Here are questions to consider:

1. when to conduct a remote oral history interview
2. what to consider when conducting a remote interview
3. documentation
4. options for recording a remote interview
5. technological options for recording a remote interview and
6. how to synch audio files.

Oral historians were not daunted by the pandemic; instead, they developed criteria for deciding whether to postpone the interviews or to conduct them remotely. In fact, oral historians have actually found some advantages to online interviewing and are currently developing best practices for doing so. The project team quickly learned that conducting military and veterans oral history interviews and designing, or even re-designing, your projects during a pandemic forces a bit more planning and preparation. Deciding very early in the process about how the interviews will be used will better help determine aspects like the most appropriate equipment to use, the location of the interviews, the mode of the interview, whether an in-person or distance format, and preservation/archival decisions. Oral historians and scholars will continue to make adjustments in order to accommodate uncertainties of a global pandemic.

Once you decide to move forward with a distance interview, additional questions and challenges arise. The safety concerns and potential loss of loved ones during the pandemic could affect the veteran's state of mind when talking about war experiences long ago. The interviewer might check the veteran's mental and physical health at this point and ask if he feels up to talking about their war experience. Another option might be to record shorter interviews rather than a life history interview.

Refer to Chapter 12: Transcribing and Archiving to learn more about oral history in the digital age. There are also additional resources about selecting the proper equipment listed in the Appendix.

Bibliography

British Oral History Society. London: Department of History, Royal Holloway, University of London. www.ohs.org.uk/covid-19-remote-recording. Accessed November 24, 2021.

MacKay, Nancy. *Curating Oral Histories: From Interview to Archive*. 2nd ed. Abingdon: Routledge, 2016.

Mann, Kim. "A Brief Guide to Basic Technology Planning for Oral History Projects." *Newsletter: Academic Technology at the College of William and Mary*. http://at.blogs. wm.edu/a-brief-guide-to-basic-technology-planning-for-oral-history-projects/. Accessed on November 15, 2021.

Oral History Association. www.oralhistory.org. Accessed November 7, 2021.

Oral History Centre – University of Winnipeg 2019. Accessed April 5, 2021 https://oralhistorycentre.ca/mobile/

10

INTERVIEWING TECHNIQUES

It is easy to assume that, when you carry on lively conversations every day, then what could be so hard about conducting an interview? In many ways that is true. A successful interview should flow like a conversation between two people, both relaxed, making eye contact, and completely engaged with each other and the topic of conversation, but there are important differences. One of them is that the interviewer and interviewee roles are quite distinct. It is not exactly a conversation. The interviewer should be in charge of interview structure, asking the questions, guiding the topics. The veteran has the information/stories that the oral history is seeking, so there is a tight, well-defined relationship between the interviewer and interviewee during the recorded interview process.

Qualities of a Good Interviewer

Although anyone can serve as an interviewer and can conduct an oral history interview with veterans, when considering your overall project design and objectives, it is always advisable to consider the qualities of a good interviewer. Veterans, sometimes but not always, make the best choice as interviewers. Barbara Sommer in *Doing Veterans Oral History* suggests pairing interviewer/interviewee according to qualities such as effectiveness working with veterans; the ability to build a trusting relationship; and the willingness to complete an in-depth and informative interview. As Sommer continues, both will have a shared understanding of experience which may lead to a more insightful interview experience. Even though they may have a difference in rank and their shared experience may result in the veteran-interviewer inserting their own experiences or lead to a more informal conversation, a veteran-interviewer may help to create a safe space and know which questions are better to ask. Other good qualities of a good interviewer may include differences and similarities in race, age, gender, ethnic background, and region (15–16).

DOI: 10.4324/9781003280323-13

Initially, I felt conflicted with my ethical responsibility to the veterans not to further distort their experiences or "mis-tell" their stories. I had to re-negotiate my sense of self as an "interpretive authority for the culture group" of Vietnam Veterans that I had worked with for years (Yow 67). While I was learning the oral history process, studying about the trauma and silence of war and preparing to document, transcribe, categorize, and classify their interviews, I never once considered what my gender would represent to these veterans during the interview. I never considered my own transformation in this process and what I had to represent in order to truly *listen to* and *hear* their stories. Stoeltje discusses how every ethnographer brings his or her historicity (the uniqueness of person) to bear on the way he or she approaches the subject, conducts the fieldwork, and resolves the interplay between the universal and the particular. My mere presence during the process was intertwined with issues of race, gender, identity, boundaries, location, and even displacement. Reflecting on one own's identity and the relation of the self to the other heightens the awareness of the ethnographer and helps to bring into focus the relationship between the researcher and the researched (158). The interviews reveal moments when the nature of my presence impeded their testimonies, so on some levels, my presence created moments of silence as well. However, I needed to establish myself as both listener and witness during the interview process and this required having an understanding of how trauma can manifest itself as silence. As the listener, I knew that I had to bear the burden of the trauma of their experiences; I had to experience at least part of their trauma for myself. I also had to be able to recognize their silence as part of their narrative structure by establishing limits and boundaries that I would not cross during the interview (see Chapter 7).

The veteran's interview process becomes even more difficult when there is not an active listener to share the experiences with them. The veterans must comprehend their own traumatic experiences before they can share their experiences with others. Most veterans have already established an implicit trust among themselves. The hardest step in building trust is always accepting a nonveteran (interviewer) into their community. Because they are sharing personal memories and revealing highly personal experiences, there must be a certain level of trust that exists between the interviewer and veteran-narrator. The listener/interviewer must be willing to become a part of the experience – to share the trauma.

Preparing for the Interview

The interviewer should conduct background research, prepare interview questions, call the veteran the day before the interview to engage the veteran, and answer any questions and reassure them if they have doubts. You may also want to discuss any general paperwork that will occur prior to the start of the interview, such as biographical data forms and consent/release forms. The interviewee may be interested in what will be asked during the interview. If you have selected not to share the interview questions with the veteran before the actual interview, then you can share general topics during the phone call.

Role of the Interviewer

As the listener, you bear the burden of the trauma of the veteran's wartime experiences. Remember the influence you could have on the interview process and offer some understanding of their attitudes and language. Be aware of your own body language and emotional responses and be willing to change the subject to avoid triggering traumatic memories. Allow space for silence and reflection. Interviewers should understand combat stress and PTSD and recognize how those traumatic experiences affect the veteran's memories, thereby affecting what they share during the interview. The interviewer must recognize how a veteran's silence during the interview about their war experiences is a significant part of their narrative (see Chapter 7).

Tips for the Interview

In order to best represent your audience, keep the purpose of the interview and the overall objective of the project in mind during the entire process. Keep the veteran focused on the specific questions asked since these are the questions that you and the audience want to know. Always respect the veteran's story and encourage the veteran to speak honestly and from the heart during the interview. Respect the boundaries established at the onset of the interview process. Remember your role as the interviewer by listening carefully and relying on background research. As the interviewer, remain compassionate and sensitive to the veteran's situation. Establish the veteran's connection to the information he provides and do not shy away from controversial and difficult topics as long as the questions respect the boundaries. Do not interrupt while the veteran is answering the questions. Do not disagree with or challenge the veteran's stories, even if you notice any discrepancies, such as dates, battle names, and locations. Respect the veteran's moments of silence (see Chapter 7) by being mindful of your own body language by using nonverbal clues to provide positive feedback, such as nodding your head in agreement, eye contact, and smiling. Pay attention to the veteran's emotions by reading body language, listening for voice cues, and watching for changes in their appearance, such as facial expressions. Pace the interview and utilize visual cues to help jog the veteran's memories. Be sure to take notes during the interview on a notepad instead of on a computer to avoid the possible distraction of typing and keep track of time and take breaks as needed.

Selecting an Interview Setting

Though practical considerations often intrude the well-being (comfort and convenience) of the interview, the veteran being interviewed should be the primary criterion in selecting the location for your interview. There are several factors to consider when interviewing war veterans.

There are three categories of settings suitable for oral history interviews: the veteran's home or other location familiar to the veteran, an office space such as the oral history project's office, or a studio setting, especially suitable for video interviews. Each setting has advantages and disadvantages. Choose a setting based on (1) the veteran's comfort in the space, and (2) a space that will suit your technology requirements. It should be a quiet place away from typical, everyday distraction. If the interviewer feels the need to have better control of the placement of equipment, recorders, microphones, and cameras, it is fine to suggest that the veteran come to you for a studio interview.

Setting Up the Space

When you arrive at the interview site, survey the room for possible obstacles. Be sure to allow time before and after the interview to manage the recording equipment. Close any doors to allow for the most privacy. The veteran may have a comfortable spot in their home in which they would prefer to conduct the interview, such as a chair, the dining room or kitchen table, a reading nook, or their own special room. If this is the case, then try to accommodate them to allow for a maximum level of comfort for the veteran. If their chosen location in the home is unsuitable because of noise, lack of electrical outlets or lighting, ask if a different part of the home might be used. The veteran may even give you a tour of the home and allow you to select the best location for the interview.

The Interviewer as Part of the Interview

Your role as the interviewer affects the outcome of the interview itself. Interviewers typically sit directly across from the interviewee. During video interviews, consider the placement and position of the camera and if the interviewer should be within the camera's frame. (It is most common practice for a single camera to focus on the interviewee.) Does it this lend itself to the question-and-answer format of the interview or does it create a conversational flow? As the interviewer, remember to identify and understand the underlying issues for the interviewee's discomfort, which may be anxiety, trauma, race/ethnicity, and gender. Have tissues handy for tears and be willing to take breaks. Do not try to find the silver lining in their experiences and do not push them to tell stories that they are not ready to tell – it could cause more discomfort or could be damaging to them.

Preparing the Interview Questions

The interview questions are essential and important to this oral history process. They should be prepared, open-ended questions that would allow the veteran to talk freely. Avoid questions that suggest "yes" or "no" answers except to get a conversation started. Questions should be neutral, thought-provoking yet compassionate, never confrontational or challenging. The main purpose is for the veteran to feel comfortable sharing. Ask questions beginning with general ones and moving to more specific. Ask the same general questions of all the veterans you are interviewing;

then move to more specific questions that to capture the nuances of each veteran's experience. This approach will provide both collective and individual wartime documentation. As you are designing your interview questions, keep your intended project goals in mind. Design the questions to seek the information relating to the overall purpose of the project. These questions are a good way to begin the interview:

1. Please state and spell your name for the record.
2. When and where were you born?
3. In which branch of the military did you serve?
4. Did you enlist or were you drafted?
5. When and where did you do your basic training?

(See the Appendix for a sample of interview questions that would be appropriate for conducting interviews with veterans.)

As I was preparing the interview questionnaire for my oral history project, "Breaking the Silence," I kept my primary goals of the project in mind. I wanted to interview Vietnam Veterans from the eastern regions of North Carolina who still resided in those small towns after the war. I had to seek out this particular population during the initial planning phrases of my project, so I had to keep these aspects as a central focus while preparing my interview questions.

Preparing for the Interview

I highly recommend meeting face to face with the veteran at least once before the recorded interview. During this initial meeting, you can ask the veteran to complete the biographical information form and maybe review the interview questions. This is the time to confirm your scheduled interview time, date, and place and to answer the veteran's concerns or questions. Make sure to exchange contact information and to remind the veteran to contact you if anything should change. This allows the veteran to feel a bit more comfortable with you and with the entire process. (During a pandemic, this initial contact may happen via a telephone call, ZOOM meeting, or video call.)

For example, while chatting with the veteran, you may discover facts about his experience that would warrant further research, such as names of battles, locations of battles, and awards received. As the interviewer, demonstrate your sincere interest in the veteran's war experiences by showing a bit of knowledge (Stoeltje 159). According to Paul Stillwell of the US Naval Institute, oral history is valued for preserving recollections of events not included in history books and official documents. The infallibility of the practice comes from distorted memories due to the passing of time, how the same event maybe remembered and perceived differently by different people and the interviewer. Veterans are more comfortable when the interviewer asks more knowledgeable questions (xxvi–xxvii.). Rely on the background research you conducted. The interviewer's research, including both biographical data about the veteran narrator and general research about the historical era, helps you to develop the interview questions and also provide a context for the interview. This research can help clarify the veteran's answers or how to deal with unexpected information.

Conducting the Interview

As interviewer, you may need to prepare yourself emotionally and psychologically for the interview with a veteran. According to Dori Laub in "Bearing Witness or the Vicissitudes of Listening," the listener to trauma comes to be a participant and a co-owner of the traumatic event: through just listening, the interviewer comes to partially experience the trauma himself. The relation of the victim to the event of the trauma, therefore, impacts on the relation of the listener to it, and the latter comes to feel the bewilderment, injury, confusion, dread, and conflicts that the trauma victim feel. He has to address all these, if he is to carry out his function as a listener (interviewer), and if trauma is to emerge, so that its henceforth impossible witnessing can indeed take place. The listener, therefore, by definition partakes of the struggle of the victim with the memories and residue of his or her traumatic past. The listener has to tell the victim's victories, defeats, and silences, know them from within, so that they can assume the form of testimony (58).

On the day of the interview, you may prepare a one-page prep list that includes the proper equipment needed for the day. Allow extra time setting up and putting away the recording equipment, greeting the interviewee, and answering his questions, or simply the interviewee's desire to chat with you before or after. Never hurry the interviewee. If you have planned for a one-hour interview, allot two hours for the actual interview and another thirty minutes for preparation time and equipment set-up. Timing for oral history interviews need not be precise. Be prepared for the interview to be either shorter or longer than you expected. Any delays or extra time taken should be because of the interviewee's needs of general circumstances, not yours. Arrive on time with all of your consent/release forms, questions, etc., and equipment, and be familiar with proper interviewing techniques and with the recording equipment (see Chapter 9).

Keeping Interview Records

Keeping accurate records for each interview is essential for good oral history practice. Information collected in the forms (see samples in the Appendix) is used by the project and/or the repository, or you can adapt the forms listed below to the parameters of your project and of the receiving archives. Checking off every step in the process, with the date accomplished, location of relevant materials, and specific notes will keep your project in line and will comply with the guidelines of the *Oral History Association*.

- Interview Questions is a list of questions to be asked during the actual interview. These consist of general questions common to the project and also questions customized to the particular interview

- Biographical data sheet will collect background information on the veteran
- Interviewer's Release/Consent Form gives permission to conduct the interview
- Veteran's Release/Consent Form gives permission to participate in the interview
- Photograph Log will list and describes any photographs provided during the project by veteran

Veterans Oral History in the Digital Age

The digital revolution has made the world both bigger, giving us access to unprecedented amounts of information and resources – and smaller, making it easier to connect with people and their stories. For better or for worse, it forces us to balance questions of transparency and privacy. The digital environment forces us to reassess our conceptions of intimacy and distance in oral history practice. "Oral historians have long-debated the balance between these two poles and technology forces us to reconsider what either can really mean in a fluid, expansive and rapidly changing context. In the digital world, intimacy is not just about the relationships between interviewer and interviewee; it is also about how digital tools allow us to actually hear the voices of the people we interview rather than relying on transcription. However, in a digital context, the seeming permanence of digitized material can too easily divorce online interviews from their contexts, their histories, and their idiosyncrasies" (Sheftel 279–280). Oral historians have long acknowledged that no matter how intimate an interview is, not everything can be said within that space, and the context of digitization compels us to acknowledge silence as a deliberate and sometimes necessary choice given the breadth and limitations of medium. While there are millions of voices on the Internet, still not everyone is represented, listened to, or even willing to put themselves out there (281).

A Case for Video Interviews

When considering the digital aspect of veterans oral history, Shizuoka and Nakemura suggest that by adding visual evidence or videos, you will capture nonverbal communication and the surroundings of your veteran. This helps in the process of capturing and documenting the complexity and nuances of the lived experiences of the veteran. It also captures the unheard, unseen and sometimes marginalized communities that are often affected by such factors as race, gender, and disabilities (see Chapter 5) because for some projects the most significant aspect centers around visibility. This can be very important for communities of color because it offers a different dynamic than the typical methodology of the oral histories when the interviewer simply ask pre-researched interview questions, then they organize the responses and create the final product. By adding the visual aspects to veterans oral history, it allows the veteran to represent themselves as they actually are and not as other's see or perceive them (29–49).

There are several advantages of modern, visual, and digital technology in veterans oral requires minimal lighting and equipment while avoiding that sense of intrusion. The cameras are more available to a larger and more diverse socioeconomic demographic to allow this type of interviewing to be more accessible to more communities. People have become more accustomed to being photographed and/or filmed in their daily lives due to the popularity of social media. There is more of a sincerity and personal investment by those behind the camera which helps the veteran speak openly and honestly. A camera can also add the presence of an audience much more so than just a tape recorder. The video provides selective information about the veteran-narrator but not an absolute record of experience. Digital technology is also more appealing and popular (Barnett and Noriega 7).

It was only after my first oral history project had been in progress for a few years that I realized the significance of the visual aspect to veterans oral history. I did very little documentation other than the tape-recorded interviews, biographical forms, and photos, if the veteran wanted to share them. Not too long after an interview with one particular veteran, he died suddenly from a heart attack. A few years after that, the very first veteran I actually interviewed and who was one of the first to agree to participate in the project died from a long battle with stomach cancer. After this, I started to incorporate more video-taping and photography into our interview sessions. By the time my father died and shortly after that, another veteran in the project died, I had completely transitioned to visual documentation. This transition created a digital database for listeners to hear those stories without having to read a full transcription. But more than, the video recordings provided the families with living testimonies from their loved ones.

Bibliography

Barnett, Teresa and Chow A. Noriega, eds. *Oral History and Communities of Color*, edited by Teresa Barnett and Chou A. Noriega. Los Angeles, CA: UCLA Chicano Studies Research Center Press, 2013, pp. 1–17.

Laub, Dori. "Bearing Witness or the Vicissitudes of Listening." *Testimony: Crisis of Witnessing in Literature, Psychoanalysis, and History*, edited by Shoshana Felman and Dori Laub. New York: Routledge, 1992, pp. 57–74.

Sheftel, Anna. "Listening to and Learning from Stories. In the Digital World." *Beyond Women's Word: Feminism and the Practices of Oral History in the University in the Twenty-First Century*, edited by Katrina Srigley, Stacey Zembrzycki and Franca Iacovetta. New York: Routledge, 2018, pp. 279–282.

Shizuoka, Karen L., and Robert Nakemura. "See What I'm Saying? Adding the Visual to Oral History." *Oral History and Communities of Color*, edited by Teresa Barnett and Chou A. Noriega. Los Angeles, CA: UCLA Chicano Studies Research Center Press, 2013, pp. 29–49.

Stoeltje, Beverly J, Christie L. Fox, and Stephen Olbrys, "The Self in 'Fieldwork': A Methodological Concern." *The Journal of American Folklore* vol. 112, no. 444, 1999, pp. 158–182. DOI: https://doi.org/10.2307/541947

Yow, Valerie. "Do I Like Them Too Much?" Effects of the Oral History Interview on the Interviewer and Vice-Versa." *Oral History Review* vol. 24, no. 1, 1997, pp. 55–79.

11

INTERVIEWING WAR VETERANS

The interviewer's relationship with the veteran is important to the process. Some veterans may request to be interviewed by a person of the same gender, race, class, military branch, and/or rank or by a particular person they know and trust? Try to honor this request. Veterans, like all of us, are often more comfortable talking to someone with whom they share a common experience. Some veterans prefer talking to another veteran, who shared the experience of participating in a war. Other veterans feel more comfortable talking to an outsider, someone unfamiliar with or outside the war experience. Those veterans may talk more freely and share more information because they may see the interview as a teaching opportunity or may not have to worry about the reactions of a family member or a familiar interviewer. If by chance, the interviewer and the veteran are related, this could affect their comfortability because of familiarity. During this process, consider how these factors may affect their comfort and how well they feel supported. Taking these factors into consideration helps strengthen the trust relationship between the interviewer and the veteran.

Identifying Veterans to Interview

Every veteran has a story worthy of telling, but not every veteran is the right one to interview at any particular time and place. Identifying veterans to interview is determined by both the (1) the capacity/interest/needs of the veteran himself and (2) the parameters of the oral history project.

The Veteran

Conducting an oral history interview with a war veteran might seem different from an interview with a nonveteran. A war veteran may be enthusiastic, reluctant, suspicious, concerned, or fearful – a whole range of emotions may be triggered at an invitation to

DOI: 10.4324/9781003280323-14

talk about their wartime experiences. There may also be practical considerations that would affect the interview: distance in time from the actual war experience, physical limitations that may limit the practicality of an interview at the time of the project, logistical limitations that make transportation to the interview site impractical, or they may be simply not ready to talk. All of these factors are simply part of landscape that the interviewer/project manager/oral historian must incorporate into the project design. Additional time may be needed for the veteran to consider their participation, especially if he has never spoken publicly about his experiences.

The Project Goals: a number of factors in the project design that would guide the choice of veteran interviewees.

1.   *Family or public project.* A family oral history project would obviously include only family members who are veterans. If you are conducting a family oral history project, then the choice is very narrow or might be a single veteran [though a family project that includes a number of veterans, of different generations and different war experiences, but become a real gem of family history]. In this case, the determining questions would be: (1) which of the family veterans are ready/willing to be interviewed? (2) Should they be interviewed separately, in a group interview, or both (some interviewing private, with additional interviewing as a group). (3) Should the interviewer be a veteran or another family member?

2.   *Project based on common experience.* Sometimes veterans' reunions are a site of oral history projects (e.g., Golden Thirteen reunion interviews – Chapter 5). When veterans gather on happy occasions to recount their wartime experience, the collective energy/memory inspires lots of wartime stories. Group interviews, though not common oral history practice, can sometimes generate positive energy and trigger memories.

3.   *Project documenting a certain war/battalion/situation.* Other oral history projects are defined by the boundaries of the project, for example, a community oral history project would include only veterans that live within a community, a women's oral history project would narrow the choice of interviewees to women, and so on. You can also build a project using more creative parameters, such as pairing veterans of different generations or wars to interview each other.

Sometimes the scope of the project automatically determines whom should be interviewed. For example, a project documenting war experience in Afghanistan, women in combat, Vietnam Veterans who were exposed to Agent Orange. These kinds of research projects narrowly define the scope of whom to interview thereby allowing you to target your interviewees.

Once you have settled on the group or cohort that defines your project, you are left with the task of finding the most appropriate interviewees. Many projects develop a pool of potential interviewees by seeking referrals from other veterans, family and friends, and veterans' organizations. You can ask veterans to complete a questionnaire and from this group, select veterans from the information they provide. The veteran must be willing to be interviewed and participate in the oral history process. The veteran needs to understand the purpose of the interview and how the material will be used. Allow the veteran sufficient time to think about participating in the interview, especially if he has never spoken publicly about his experiences. You can work through veterans' organizations or community partners for referrals of veterans who may be willing to participate in an interview. Some veterans may be willing to participate but only in a group setting or in writing, through emails or letters. These types of interviews allow them to feel more comfortable with the process. Even if a veteran agrees to be interviewed, he may choose not to share some memories or answer questions that may trigger traumatic or painful memories. Older generations of veterans, World War II, Korean, Vietnam, Cold War, First Persian Gulf War/Desert Storm, and other conflicts, may be more willing to share their experiences due to the passing of time than the recent war veterans. A veteran may agree to participate in an interview but is only willing to be interviewed by either another veteran (maybe even of the same rank), someone of the same gender, age, race/ethnicity, or someone with similar religious, political, educational, or geographical backgrounds. A veteran may be more comfortable talking to a complete stranger about their war experiences. A veteran may not want to be interviewed by a family member; may have a disability that impairs hearing, vision, or both; may have either diagnosed PTSD or undiagnosed PTSD, given the age of the veteran; and may also have physical conditions that may affect the interview.

Revisiting the Human Factor

Be sure to acknowledge the perceived the state-of-mind of the veteran. As discussed in Chapter 6 Trust, Trauma, and the Human Factor, traumatic memories are challenging issues that may arise during interviews. This may not be the case for every veteran, but it is definitely worth keeping in mind. During your initial meeting with the veteran, you can ask if there is anything that he specifically does not want be asked about. Even on the day of the interview, remind the veteran that they can stop the interview at any time or say that there is a question he does not want to answer. During the interview, be respectful and mindful that this could happen so being prepared to move to the next question or stop the interview momentarily or entirely for that day. This is the time that your patience, understanding, and compassion will be most needed. The veteran may even choose to continue to talk but ask not to be recorded. Honor this request and promptly turn off all recording equipment. Allowing time to move through the discomfort or traumatic memory may be what is needed for the veteran to continue with the recorded interview. If he chooses not to continue at that time, then ask if he would like to talk about this experience at a later time, and if he agrees, be sure to follow up. When the interview is over, it may prove beneficial to stay in contact with the veteran just in case you need to conduct follow-up interview or request additional information. Remain in contact with the veteran(s) at least through the completion of your project. Once initial interviews are completed, you may need additional information or to conduct a follow-up interview. Also, you would want to keep the veteran participants abreast of your project's developments, events, and other activities. Be sure to contact them once their interviews have been transcribed, edited, excerpted, or digitally formatted (depending on your project's outcomes), so they can review their own interviews before they are released for public access. This will give both of you time to make any changes.

Different Ways of Interviewing Veterans

There are different types of interviews that might be more appropriate for veterans oral history projects, depending on your specific project design. These are all important documentary techniques and can be used either on their own or in conjunction with traditional oral history interviews.

Private Family interviews in which compiling family history is one of the main reasons why people conduct oral history interviews of their veteran relatives. This is a great way to preserve the family's military legacy, provide information for end-of-life events (such as the veteran's wishes about memorials, funerals, and obituaries), and give the veteran an honored place in the family history. A private family interview has both similarities and differences between an interview conducted for a public audience and preserved in a public repository.

In 2009, I was approached after a conference presentation in which I showed a short digital story in which my father was discussing his time in Vietnam and living with PTSD. A young lady approached me after the presentations and asked, "that video reminded me of my two uncles who served in both the Korean and Vietnam wars. My mother also served as a nurse during the Vietnam War. I should probably interview them, right?" I responded, "yes, you should, if they are willing." She continued, "but what if I do not have a project for the interview once I have recorded it?" I simply responded, "record the interview. Document the story, so at least you will have it. You can decide what to do with it later. If they are willing to let you record their stories now, go for it." During that moment, I condensed the most important steps when conducting private family interviews with veterans. These steps may be similar to conducting an institution or community project but are still important to follow:

- Conduct the interview even if you do not have any specific intentions for the interview at the beginning.
- Record on simple household devices, such as a smartphone or tablet. You can record in audio only or audio and video.
- Begin the recorded interview with an introductory script specifying your name and the veteran's name, the date (including year) and place of the interview. This will become important later if you decide to contribute the interview to a public repository.
- Get the veteran's verbal consent on the audio or video recorder by asking the veteran to state and spell his full name and to answer the following question: do I have your consent to record your interview today?

- As soon as possible after the interview, transfer the digital file to a trusted hard drive for safe keeping. Make digital copies as backups.
- Ask questions even if you know the answers.
- Ask open-ended questions. Let the veteran tell his story. Don't fill in the blanks unless he asks for help. Keep questions neutral. Don't judge. Don't try to steer the veteran's story into an overly positive, overly negative view of their war experiences.

Life History Interview. According to Hugo Slim and Paul Thomson in "Ways of Listening," life story interviews are normally private, one-to-one encounters between interviewer and interviewee. Sessions should be held at a time convenient to the interviewee and in a suitable location, preferably somewhere which offers seclusion, comfort, and familiarity. The best place for this type of interview is the veteran's home. It is common for life story interviews to be conducted over multiple sessions and can take from one to eight hours. Breaking the interview into separate sessions gives people time to remember and explore the past and makes recollecting more of a process than an occasion. It lessens the pressure of a single interview session. Memories triggered in one session can be reflected upon by the narrator in peace and then resumed during the next interview session. This method emphasizes that a participant has rarely if ever been asked to recall their entire life in the course of a few hours. The interviewer should make sure that the participant is comfortable and feels supported as these interviews can be positive and quite emotional experiences in which they gain satisfaction and a renewed sense of perspective about their life (145–146).

The single-issue interview seeks to gain testimony about a veteran's experiences during an event or episode such as conflict or war. It may be carried out on a one-to-one or group basis and focus on a specific aspect of the veteran's life. They can be shorter than a life story but more detailed. This interview is the main method of documenting a particular event, requiring the interviewer to have a more thorough knowledge of the subject matter than is necessary for a more wide-ranging life story (145–146).

Diary interviewing involves selecting a sample of people who contribute regular diary entries as a part of a continuing and long-term study of social trends. The project may ask people to report on specific issues or it might seek more general life story material. The participants make a commitment to keep a written or oral tape-recorded diary. Entries may be on a daily, weekly, monthly or annual basis and then analyzed over time. Alternatively, diary interviewing can involve a less rigorous procedure whereby the participant is interviewed at key moments over a period of time. The objectives of diary interviewing are therefore to collect a running progress of a person's experience over time and not just retrospectively (146–147).

Group interviews (group conversations) public meetings may be more familiar and oral testimony collection can be adapted accordingly. However, groups can bring out the best and worst in people. By taking the focus off of the individual, it makes them feel less inhibited but the opposite can occur just as easily. Group

members can also spark off one another. Memories are triggered, facts can be verified or checked, views can be challenged and the burning issues of the past can be
discussed and argued about in the light of the present. Group interviewing can also
help establish rapport between the interviewer/project team and the veteran community,
encouraging people to come forward for one-to-one sessions if appropriate. Two
types of group interviewing are appropriate for oral history collections: *Small focus-
group discussions* and *larger community interviews.*

Small focus group discussions are useful for discussing both the past and major
events of the day. They are especially helpful for collecting testimony from people
who may be very reserved on a one-to-one basis but gain confidence from being
in a group, such as war veterans. This method brings between five and twelve
people together to discuss a particular issue or a number of issues. They should be
a homogeneous group made up of participants of the same gender and equal in
social status, knowledge, and experience so that confidence is high and no one feels
threatened. The discussion should last one or two hours, with participants sitting
comfortably in a circle facing each other. Multiple sessions can be held if necessary. The main emphasis in this method is the interaction between the participants
themselves and not the interaction between the participants and the interviewer.
A moderator instead of the interviewer may guide the focus group. The moderator's
role is to steer the discussion and ask probing questions. While group interviews
may prove to be more difficult to orchestrate, the presence of other veterans in the
group might help by jogging participants' memories and helping others remember
dates, times, places, and events. Group interviews may also present challenges during transcriptions because it may be difficult to distinguish one voice from another,
if these group sessions are not videotaped. The interviewer will also fall into the
role of moderator during a group interview in order to give everyone ample time
to speak and so no one can monopolize the interview process (146–147).

Community interviews involve larger groups and may resemble public meetings
more than group discussions. The emphasis in a community interview is on the
main interaction between the interviewer and the community. The ideal size is
around thirty people and two interviewers will be needed so if the interview runs
long, one interviewer can take a break. Interviewers may even take turns asking
questions to the group. Their role is to directly ask the interview questions while
still taking responsibility for balancing participation in the meeting with guiding
the interview. The two interviewers should define their respective roles before the
process and ensure that they do not speak at the same time or interrupt each other's
line of questioning. This method is an opportunity to gather a wide cross section
of people together at one time. This is useful at the start of a project for collecting background information or for future interviews. It is also a useful method in
the middle of your project or at the end of the interviewing process when certain
details or views need to be checked or verified (148).

Keep in mind that the veterans oral history interview may impact the family.
Families may not be prepared to hear or be able to understand their veteran's full
story, so it is advisable not to have family members present during the interview

unless the veteran makes that specific request. Since family members know each other so well, the interview may become conversational. Conversations are back-and-forth discussions, an interchange of thoughts and ideas. Interviews with veterans should be directed question-and-answer sessions. The interviewer asks open-ended questions and listens while the veteran answers them. If the interview becomes conversational, which may happen if a veteran interviews a veteran, try not to become overly involved by forgetting the purpose of the interview.

Bibliography

Slim, Hugo, and Paul Thomson. "Ways of Listening" *The Oral History Reader*, edited by Robert Perks and Alistair Thomson. New York: Routledge, 1998.

IV

After the Interview

12

TRANSCRIBING AND ARCHIVING

After the Interview

The purpose in doing veterans oral history interviews – for family enjoyment, for a community event to honor veterans, or simply to produce a research document, influence the decisions you make in the planning and implementation of an oral history project and steps required after the interview – in cataloging, preservation, and access. Donald Ritchie poses the following questions to consider once the interviews are complete:

- What constitutes the boundaries of the community?
- How broadly or narrowly do we want to define our audience?
- Did interviewees expect their life stories to remain relatively unused except by the occasional scholar, or did they hope to leave something of themselves for posterity, where their memories might be published, exhibited, and otherwise not forgotten? (14).

For example, family interviews should be carefully labeled and digital copies made. They do not need a signed legal consent form unless they will be contributed to a public archives but family members may include photos and accompanying documents in a "package" that will become a family keepsake. On the other hand, researchers intending to use the interviews for publication will need a signed legal release form giving permission from the narrator for his words to be used. If the interview is intended to go into a library as well, then additional steps must be taken in the language of the legal release form, recording quality to the library's standards. An information sheet such as the Interview Summary form (see example in the Appendix) should accompany the interview to the library. Nancy MacKay's *After the Interview in Community Oral History* Volume 5 provides excellent tips on

DOI: 10.4324/9781003280323-16

processing, transcribing, cataloging, preservation, access, and closing out the project and the oral history interviews just conducted and collected.

Transcribing

Ritchie suggests that if transcribing the interviews is not possible, then the project should at least consider including an abstract along with the biographical data sheet and contextual information that may help a listener better understand the recording. Oral historians usually decide whether interviews will be transcribed when the project is planned, because of the added expense involved. If so, they need add transcription to the budget, time frame, and staffing needs. For a complete description of transcription issues, consult *Transcribing Oral History*, by Teresa Bergen (Routledge, 2020). In summary, transcribing choices are:

1. Transcribe within the by project team, interviewer, or another person;

    a. Pros: Transcriber invested in the project, may know the interviewee, more likely to understand speech patterns of interviewee, usually less expensive
    b. Cons: Lack professional standards

2. Outsourcing to professional transcriber

    a. Pros: Quicker, professional transcript
    b. Cons: Transcriber does not have the inside knowledge of the topic, more expensive

3. Instead of a full transcription, create an interview summary, including topics discussed, names of wars/conflicts, dates, and personal names

    a. Pros: Quicker, cheaper, and serves the purpose for general access
    b. Cons: Does not capture the interviewee's speech patterns or the complete story

Archiving

Most oral histories are created for the public, historical record, that is, for research, education, and enjoyment far into the future. In order for that to happen the oral histories need to be deposited to a repository (library or archives) for safe keeping and access. Some oral history projects are part of an archives so the task is automatic; other projects, such as community-based projects must make an arrangement with the repository, preferable before the project begins. Do not expect repositories to accept your oral histories automatically. See Nancy MacKay's *Curating Oral Histories*, 2nd ed. (Routledge, 2016) for a full discussion.

Though archiving in a permanent repository is an important step in the oral history life cycle, it may not always be the right choice for veterans oral histories. Occasionally veterans will be interviewed informally, as part of a family gathering to share only for that moment, as part of a therapy group or veterans reunion, or even as part of a focus group in preparation for a formal oral history project. This is completely fine. No matter what the purpose, it is essential that the veterans being interviewed understand exactly what will happen to their recording, and that they have control over the oral history process at every step. Archiving options range from a small but organized archive accessible only to members of a family or small group all the way up to a to a large repository such as the *Library of Congress Veterans History Project*.

The decision about archiving interviews should be made during the project design and preparation stages (see Chapter 8), and the specific steps for archiving are determined by the agreement between your project and the repository. Remember that oral historians cannot simply deposit their interviews into repository. There are often set terms and conditions that are determined by the repository itself before this can occur. If your project is being conducted under the auspices of a library, university, historical society, archival facility, or other research institutions, oral history interviews in a place that is equipped to preserve the interviews for public use and availability. Or your project may be conducted as an individual or small project with the intention of donating them to a larger project. For example, the *Veterans History Project* at the Library of Congress accepts donated interviews. Institutions closer to home, like local public libraries and community centers may take donated interviews that reflect experiences of members of their own community. Sometimes, though, things in life do not follow such an orderly path. A great recording with a veteran may show up in a box when cleaning out the closet or a recorded dinner table conversation turns out to be so interesting and informative that the family decides the local library would be interested in making it available. If you are lucky, the veteran is nearby to give his consent (if not, the family can act in his best interests). All of these situations happen in real life and need to be addressed on a case-by-case basis with the veteran's best wishes in mind.

Considering the human factor discussed in Chapters 6, soon after the interview, consider sending a written or personalized thank you note to the veteran acknowledging participation, reminding them of the goal for the recorded interview. Make the recording (audio/video/CD) available soon after the interview was conducted for the purpose of memorials, funerals, etc. – then provide an edited copy/version later (including transcriptions). Depending on the intended purpose of the interview, the interviewer must be fully committed to the process of editing, transcribing, preserving for future use, and/or making available for access.

Bibliography

Bergen, Teresa. *Transcribing Oral History*. New York: Routledge, 2020.

Boyd, Douglas A. and Mary A. Larson, Eds. *Oral History and Digital Humanities: Voice, Access and Engagement*. New York: Palgrave McMillan, 2014.

MacKay, Nancy. *After the Interview in Community Oral History* Volume 5 (in the *Community Oral History Toolkit*). Walnut Creek, CA: Left Coast Press, 2013.

MacKay, Nancy. *Curating Oral Histories: From Interview to Archive*. New York: Routledge, 2016.

Oral History Association. www.oralhistory.org. Accessed November 7, 2021.

Ritchie, Donald. *Doing Oral History. A Practical Guide*. New York: Oxford UP, 2003.

The Veterans History Project at the Library of Congress. www.loc.gov/vets. Accessed November 7, 2021.

13
USING VETERANS ORAL HISTORY

After the veterans oral history project is complete, it is ready to be enjoyed and used for various purposes, from research to visual arts projects. There are several products that may emerge from your work. Veterans oral history can be shared as collections and projects through print, mixed media, digital, and teaching resources. It is important to ensure the accessibility of materials for the veterans themselves and ensure their comfort level with their shared stories. According to Paul Thompson in *The Voice of the Past*, there are four ways that oral history can be interpreted:

1. Single life-story narrative: used to convey the history of a whole class or community or become a thread around which to reconstruct a highly complex series of events.
2. Collection of stories: better represent more typical life-history material and allows the stories to be used much more easily in constructing a broader historical interpretation by grouping them – as a whole or fragmented – around common themes.
3. Narrative analysis: the focus is on the interview itself as an oral test and what can be learned from its language, its themes and repetitions and its silences. It is concerned with how the narrator experienced, remembered, and retold his or her life-story, and what light this may throw on the consciousness of the wider society. It does not normally aim to evaluate the typicality of the narrator or his or her experiences.
4. Reconstructive cross-analysis: the oral evidence is treated as a quarry from which to construct an argument about patterns of behavior or events in the past (269–270).

DOI: 10.4324/9781003280323-17

Books

When people first started interviewing veterans, often such collaborations resulted in oral history books with either completely or partially transcribed interviews intermingled with the author's commentary, without any reader access to the audio recordings. Most books could include only a sampling of the interviews, often with a thematic approach carefully orchestrated by the editor of the collection. For example, Al Santoli's book, *Everything We Had: An Oral History of the Vietnam War* (1981), focuses on more than just retrieving, providing and preserving information but also on representing human experiences in times and places that are unfamiliar to the reader. When veterans oral histories are obtained and published, private and public therapies merge, reintegrating experience into the individual and the national consciousness (Bennett 5, 12). A regional oral history by Stanley W. Beesley, *Vietnam: The Heartland Remembers* (1988), focuses on a select group of Oklahomans who served in Vietnam. He recorded their experiences in a manner which allowed the testimonies to be spontaneous. He published the testimonies as they were told, with slang and military terminology in hopes of properly conveying the accuracy and authenticity of their stories (7). Yvonne Latty in *We Were There: Voices of African American Veterans from World War II to the War in Iraq* (2012) focuses her oral history collection on the complexity of how African Americans defeated two enemies simultaneously: racism and war. Her interest and curiosity, like my own, developed from her own father's service in World War II, leading her to question how her father could serve a country that discriminated against him because of his race. While her collection pulled from some previously collected oral histories by others, she intentionally focused on the African American race across several generations of wars. Oral history books, even on the past war generations, are still being published. William Brinker's edited collection, *And We Did Cope: Stories of Thirty-Six Wives, Fiancées, Mothers, Daughters, and Sisters of Men Who Served in Vietnam* in 2012, focused on stories of the women who supported loved ones who fought in Vietnam and the ways the war affected those left behind. He used the oral history interviews of thirty-six women who were willing, in fact, anxious to participate. These women, who were wives of career Army and Air Force officers, enlisted and drafted soldiers and Marines whose veterans served from the early 1960s to 1973 were very forthcoming with details, some unexpected and potentially embarrassing. They believed that something of this sort (the oral history collection of stories) had already been done. They expressed their appreciation for the chance to have their say to an interested listener who could share their stories with a wider audience.

Theater

Since the 1980s, veterans oral history has been used for theatrical productions. For example, "Tracers," whose title references the tracer bullets released during war, evolved from the oral histories of eight Vietnam Veterans, who also appeared in the original production. "Many of the play's segments are straightforward oral history, but such was the nature of Vietnam that its oral history will always have an arresting ring. When the soldiers describe their adventures in the jungle or in Saigon bordellos, they do so in a jivey, at times funny, language that combines timeless military lingo with rock-and-roll cadences, drug jargon, pidgin Vietnamese and English and an almost surreal litany of profanity. It's an authentic form of stylized diction, ideal for the theater, that few playwrights could invent from scratch." The play defies the stereotypes of war by the straightforward approach of the oral histories and is still being performed in various locations today. At its peak, it was under the direction of John DiFusco and the New York Vietnam Veterans Ensemble Theater Company. Over the years, the play has traveled and been directed and performed by a multitude of war veterans and citizens. I saw a performance of "Tracers" in the early 2000s in a local playhouse in Charlotte, North Carolina. The production attracted a following of local Vietnam Veterans who attended the play every night of its performance and had become very familiar with the dialogue as well as the characters.

Since 2008, "The Telling Project," a nonprofit organization in Austin, Texas, has continued to connect the past to the present through theatrical performances. The project collaborates with individuals, local community organizations, theatre departments, colleges and universities, veteran organizations to interview veterans and their family members about the military. These interviews are video-recorded, transcribed and constructed into a script that performers have the opportunity to revise. After the interview process, those veterans and their family members work directly with a theatre director. After about four to eight weeks of performance training, the result is called "Telling." The Telling Project promotes the performance in collaboration with the communities in which they work and since their inception, they have produced twenty-seven original performances in sixteen different states. These performances have included over 150 veterans and their family members in these "Telling" performances.

Film/Documentaries

The Ken Burns documentary, *The Vietnam* War (2017), is a 10-part, 18-hour documentary series, in which Burns collaborated Lynn Novick, to create a series of episodes that "aims to provide a new perspective on the United States' involvement in Vietnam by centering the stories of combatants, protesters and other witnesses, while sidelining the voices of politicians and personalities who dominated the news at the time." The documentary project included "emotional first-person interviews with people from all sides (including more than two dozen Vietnamese, from both the winning and losing sides)" ("How Ken Burns Edited The Vietnam War Documentary").

As veterans oral history continues to develop and grow, best practices must evolve to keep up with the digital revolution and the public's expectation for immediate access to documents and materials not just for research purposes but also for personal reasons.

Research Collections

Long before VHP and the digital revolution in the field of oral history, local communities and organizations were collecting veterans oral history, though on a much smaller scale. These collections typically resulted in archival collections at research facilities or universities as well as smaller local historical societies and public libraries. With the increased acceptance of oral history as a legitimate methodology for collecting and interpreting history, much of it thanks to the work of the Oral History Association (OHA) and the growing interdisciplinarity of the field, emerging scholarship and best practices within the field are constantly evolving not only to include multiple wars but to also be more inclusive of gender, race, ethnicity, and region. For example, the Betty H. Carter Women Veterans Historical Project (WVHP) founded and established at the University of North Carolina at Greensboro (UNCG) in 1998, documents the contributions of women in the military and related service organizations from World War I, World War II, the Korean War, the Vietnam War, the Cold War, Desert Storm, the Gulf Wars, and the War on Terror. It currently holds 550 collections with 350 oral histories. Beyond oral histories, these collections also include photographs, letters, diaries, scrapbooks, oral histories, military patches and insignia, uniforms, and posters as well as published works. From its inception, the goal of the project is to collect and preserve unique and rare historical materials that document the experiences of women in the US military and American Red Cross, while promoting the educational and research use of these materials by members of the university, the scholarly community, and the general public. In 2002, WVHP began to digitize the collection in order to increase functionality of the searchable database and have better access to oral histories and other documents.

Collaborations

The most rapid emerging scholarship in veterans oral history is the increase of collaborations among organizations. *VHP* and even the military began collaborations in order to collect as many war experiences as possible. For example, *The Women Marines Association* (WMA) collaborated with the Oral History Unit of the History Division of the Marine Corp by interviewing their own membership and depositing the recordings in the official Marine Corps Oral History Collection. As of 2005, they had donated over 100 oral histories to the Oral History Collection. American Veterans for Equal Rights (AVER) is another collaborative effort. It is estimated that there have been more than 65,000 gay and lesbian personnel serving on active duty and in the reserves since World War II that were not able to share their stories or their identities because of the "Don't Ask, Don't Tell" policy of 1993–1994. Since 2000, AVER is an official partner in the VHP. These oral histories explore several themes underlying the debate about homosexuality and military service: (1) the relationship between racism and homophobia in the military; (2) varying attitudes about military service within gay communities; (3)

contrasting experiences of gay men and lesbians in the military; and (4) the evolving nature of gay veterans' identities (Estes 21). Both collections are that are accessible to the public

Veterans Oral History for Social Justice

Veterans oral history, according to Sarah Loose, has both limitations and benefits for affecting social change and social movements. Even though veterans oral history takes time, it is considered a mostly private encounter and the one-on-one experience may not immediately lend itself well to a collective impact; it is a more of a generative process that helps raise questions, create and record powerful narratives and foster relationship opposed to an immediate process that can translate the narratives into action; and it produces very specific knowledge opposed to more generalize and quantifiable data (236–237). There are benefits to how it works well for social justice.

Oral history can help with understanding the history of communities and/or issues as well as understanding the causes of contemporary problems. It is often the only format in which the histories of marginalized communities and social movements can be documented. And made accessible, particularly in cases where people and communities cannot, do not, or simply will not interact with written texts. Oral history can also de-mystify the process of organizing what worked and did not work in the past. They can provide insight into individual world views, value systems, and historical consciousness as well as s wider processes and moments of transformations that can further movement building and support organizers by providing access to how individuals make sense of their history and the world.

Oral history can contribute to social justice and social movements because organizers recognize the power of how a story can shape opinions, impart lessons and mobilize services for social movements (237). Organizers recognize the power of story to shape opinions, impart lessons and mobilize in the service of justice movements (237). Social movements are moving from single-issue campaigns to values-based approaches rooted in a recognition of the intersectionality inherent in oral histories. For example, veteran projects like *The Golden Thirteen* and *When Janey Comes Marching Homes* that are recording and sharing interviews with individuals with particular experiences or identities but whose narratives reflect complicated stories about place, belonging, intimacy, violence, and corporeality. Adds texture and nuance to related social movement-oriented research and organizing efforts. Social movements can employ stories from oral history interviews "to communicate the nature and moral legitimacy of their struggle and mobilizes allies" (237). Oral histories affective engagement attributes can foster relationships and the collective identity and emotional connections that facilitate and sustain collective action. This connection can lead to social change by building identification between listeners and movements. The affective content of an oral history interview can evoke outrage, compassion, and empathy in a listener and in the process compel action (239).

Because of oral history's capacity for relationship building that can become intergenerational and enduring, it has a powerful ability for social change and movement building. Formal and intentional use of oral history interviews can augment or accelerate the process of relationship building that occurs within social movements to build trust and solidarity among the participants (240–241).

Bibliography

American Veterans for Equal Rights (AVER). https://aver.us. Accessed November 15, 2021.

Bennett, James, "Human Values in Oral History." *The Oral History Review* vol. 11, 1983, pp. 5–12.

Bessley, Stanley W. *Vietnam: The Heartland Remembers.* Norman: Univ. of Oklahoma Press, 1988.

Brinker, William Brinker. *And We Did Cope: Stories of Thirty-Six Wives, Fiancées, Mothers, Daughters, and Sisters of Men Who Served in Vietnam.* Xlibris Corporation, 2012.

Estes, Steve, "Ask and Tell: Gay Veterans, Identity, and Oral History on a Civil Rights Frontier." *Oral History Review* vol. 32, no. 2, 2005, pp. 21–47.

"How Ken Burns Edited The Vietnam War Documentary." www.masterclass.com/articles/how-ken-burns-edited-the-vietnam-war-documentary#what-is-ken-burns-the-vietnam-war. Accessed on November 25, 2021.

Latty, Yvonne. *We Were There: Voices of African American Veterans From World War II to the War in Iraq.* New York: HarperCollins, 2012.

Loose, Sarah K. and Amy Starecheski. "Oral History for Building Social Movements, Then and Now." *Beyond Women's Words: Feminisms and the Practices of Oral History in the Twenty-First Century,* edited by Katrina Srigley, Stacey Zembrzycki, and Franca Iacovetta. New York: Routledge, 2018.

Rich, Frank. "Stage: 'Tracers,' Drama of Vietnam Veterans." *New York Times,* January 22, 1985. www.nytimes.com/1985/01/22/theater/stage-tracers-drama-of-vietnam-veterans.html.

Ritchie, Donald. *Doing Oral History. A Practical Guide.* New York: Oxford UP, 2003.

Santoli, Al. *Everything We Had: Am Oral History of the Vietnam War.* New York: Random House, 1981.

Schuessler, Jennifer. "Ken Burns and Lynn Novick Tackle the Vietnam War." *The New York Times,* September 1, 2017.www.nytimes.com/2017/09/01/arts/television/ken-burns-and-lynn-novick-tackle-the-vietnam-war.html. Accessed November 24, 2021.

The Betty H. Carter Women Veterans Hospital Project (WVHP). http://libcdm1.uncg.edu/cdm/abouttheproject/collection/WVHP. Accessed November 15, 2021.

The Telling Project. www.thetellingproject.org. Accessed November 15, 2021.

The Women Marines Association (WMA). www.womenmarines.org. Accessed November 15, 2021.

Thompson, Paul Thompson. *The Voice of the Past: Oral History.* New York: Oxford UP, 2000.

14

THE VALUE OF VETERANS ORAL HISTORY

Contributions to Society's Understanding of Wartime Experiences

Veterans oral history projects and collections contribute to a deeper understanding of how veterans view their own participation in America's wars; how they have made meaning and contextualize those experiences; and how these shared experiences have affected the lives of its practitioners and communities. Harold McMillion, the former Group Leader of the Greenville Veterans Outreach Center (Vet Center), shared:

> When Sharon solicited my support in coordinating efforts in bringing a forum to campus, "Breaking the Silence: The Unspoken Brotherhood of Vietnam Veterans," it raised an issue because most Vietnam veterans avoided discussing their combat experience with anyone, which posed a true challenge. How could we recruit enough veterans and convince them to volunteer for this unique program? The purpose of the program was discussed among the Vet Center PTSD combat vet groups. The protocol was established for interviews and initial plans developed for four community forums. The overall response from the Vietnam Veterans was unbelievable. Many Vietnam Veterans viewed this opportunity as a way to tell their personal stories. This program was not only informative to the community but also formed the basis of emotional healing. The old psychic scars hidden through the years by emotional numbing began to open up and drain. Vietnam Veterans faced their community eyeball to eyeball, telling their stories with vigor, openness and raw courage. The response from the campus community and questions to Vietnam Veterans were filmed and recorded during the sessions. Veterans left the program with a deep sense of pride and satisfaction: My story was told, someone listened, and I can be at peace with myself after

DOI: 10.4324/9781003280323-18

thirty years. "Breaking the Silence: The Unspoken Brotherhood of Vietnam Veterans" is a model for other programs that want to deal with our nation's warriors. The Vet Center was honored to be a vital part of this program. The historical record of the Vietnam War was tainted by an unpopular political action. By focusing on the negative aspects of the Vietnam experience, society overlooked the personal sacrifices made by more than three million of its young men and ten thousand of its women. "Breaking the Silence" highlighted detailed individual histories, each of which is a story of monumental significance."

(17–19).

Contributions to Post-Traumatic Growth

Veterans oral history can also contribute to what is known as post-traumatic growth (PTG). PTG is a positive change experienced as a result of the struggle with a major life crisis or a traumatic event and has evolved into theory that explains this kind of transformation following trauma. It was developed by psychologists Richard Tedeschi, PhD, and Lawrence Calhoun, PhD, in the mid-1990s, and holds that people who endure psychological struggle following adversity can often see positive growth afterward. PTG tends to occur in five general areas. In the first stage, sometimes people who must face major life crises develop a sense that new opportunities have emerged from the struggle, opening up possibilities that were not present before. A second area is a change in relationships with others. Some people experience closer relationships with some specific people, and they can also experience an increased sense of connection to others who suffer. A third area of possible change is an increased sense of one's own strength – "if I lived through that, I can face anything." A fourth aspect of PTG experienced by some people is a greater appreciation for life in general. The fifth area involves the spiritual or religious domain. Some individuals experience a deepening of their spiritual lives; however, this deepening can also involve a significant change in one's belief system. Most of us, when we face very difficult losses or great suffering, will have a variety of highly distressing psychological reactions. Just because individuals experience growth does not mean that they will not suffer. Distress is typical when we face traumatic events. PTG is not universal. It is not uncommon, but neither does everybody who faces a traumatic event experience growth (19–24).

There has also been an increase in the use of oral history in readjustment counseling and community support for veterans. Clark Smith in "Oral History as 'Therapy,'" discusses how the use of oral history during counseling sessions with war veterans can be beneficial to recovery and readjustment. The actual oral history interview reverses the role of the time factor by placing the veteran in the immediacy of the experience; it allows the personality of the veteran to emerge; and it emphasizes the "war" as problematic rather than the veteran as disturbed.

"The veteran who tells his story does so with the tacit permission to unburden himself, to tell all and conceal nothing. For many veterans, the oral historical interview provides the means of memorial self-affirmation, which functions largely as a symbolic statement that they are not defeated but rather that they are contenders" (17–19). The oral history interviews generally take the focus off of the veteran and his actions and place it on the war.

Narrative therapies are becoming more prevalent in the treatment of survivors of trauma. "Coping with Traumatic Memories" discusses how narrative therapies "require repeated verbalization of traumatic memories to encourage habituation to the traumatic elements of the memory of and the integration of flashbacks into the fragmented and dissociated narrative, which leads to the remission of the traumatic symptoms through coherent narrative" (58). This type of therapy sounds complicated but a very similar version takes place regularly at Veterans Outreach Centers for readjustment counseling in which sessions are facilitated by a professional and the veterans feel comfortable and safe enough to share traumatic experiences within both one-on-one and group sessions. The oral history interviewing process allows space for those veterans who survived traumatic wartime experiences to verbally express those memories. The more they talk about their experiences, their more it may contribute to their overall growth and readjustment. Several veterans involved in all of my oral history projects were already seeking readjustment counseling through a veterans outreach center and were encouraged to participate in opportunities that allowed them to continue to share their experiences with others.

Future for Veterans Oral History

With our country's most recent wars and conflicts, there is an emergence of special issues like moral injury, polytrauma, and traumatic brain injury that may affect storytelling. The more recent war veterans returning from Iraq and Afghanistan may be more or less willing to share their experiences depending on the amount of time that has passed since their service and their combat. Veterans oral history, as a research tool, has seen an increased use in colleges and universities, particularly in doctoral dissertations, undergraduate curriculum, secondary, middle, and earlier grades (primary school) as well as among populations with heavy minority enrollment.

Veterans oral history projects organized around a college curriculum work best with community involvement that connects students with the local veteran community as well as bridging the gap between the campus community and the veteran population. These projects can emphasize generational differences of students, faculties, and veterans. Strategies that educators often use to teach the methodology of oral history may involve readings to introduce students to the use and practice of oral history in modern scholarship, watching good interviewers at work, which is a visual strategy, observing and critiquing interviews, understanding socioeconomic, race, and gender politics and issues involved in oral history.

Veterans Oral History in the Digital Age

Scholars are making cases for big possibilities for oral history in the digital age. "We now have incredible technologies that can disseminate oral history to a global audience almost instantaneously. Archives that once boasted hundreds of annual users of their collections now regularly track thousands of uses of their oral history interviews all over the world. Media outlets offer near instant and free distribution of audio and video oral histories, while digital repository and content management systems provide powerful infrastructure for housing oral histories in a digital archive or library" (Boyd and Larson).

What does that mean for veterans oral history? For starters, it means lots more ways to share veterans' stories to a broad audience, through a multitude of audio and video presentations, mostly and now over the Internet. There are several digital media veterans projects that incorporate veterans oral history that are worth considering as models if you are working in that arena. For example, "From Combat to Kentucky (C2Ky)," is a digital oral history archive of twenty-four individual video interviews with student veterans. These projects are very similar to my *Silence of War* transmedia documentary project in which oral history is incorporated into the overall project design.

Digital collections, such as *VOCES Oral History Project*, document the wartime experiences and contributions of US Latinos and Latinas during World War II, Korean War, and Vietnam War. Since its inception in 1999 by the University of Texas at Austin, journalism professor Maggie Rivas-Rodriguez has expanded from an initial focus on the World War II era to include the Korean and Vietnam eras by 2010. With the creation of the website, the oral history interviews were transcribed and listed thematically for viewers to search. The website includes oral history training materials (videos and guidelines), stories, and photographs. The project's efforts include volunteers who conduct and submit interviews. Some volunteers even cover the costs of processing, transcribing, and preparing the materials for the website. *VOCES* also operates on grant funding and donations.

A large oral history digital database, the *Witness to War* Foundation (WTW) is a nonprofit organization that also collaborates and donates their full-length interviews to VHP. The WTW Foundation was created to capture the stories of combat veterans in high-definition digital video that is inclusive of all wars to teach future generations about the combat experience. WTW records the interviews with veterans and then edit them into 2–5 minute segments or "war stories" so they are more easily accessible by all generations. Since 2002, it has captured over 1,500 stories from veterans of World War II, Korea, Vietnam, Panama, Grenada, Iraq, Afghanistan, and other conflicts. Digitally, the combat stories are thematically organized by each individual war and the database also includes photographs and memoirs.

The Internet provides numerous opportunities for researchers and communities to both hear and read oral history interviews. As oral history moves more toward digitalization of recorded materials, authors and editors must have interesting ways to write about and publish in book format collected veterans oral history. Without the nuances of the recorded voice, the oral history interview, in its transcribed format, may not continue to reach wide audiences or connect with younger generations. Because equipment standards and technological advances are constantly changing, visit the Oral History Association website to better understand oral history in the digital age and what suggestions that are listed for digital recorders and microphones.

The digital revolution, of course, informs the current practice of collecting and disseminating veterans oral history. As VHP has dedicated a tremendous amount of time and resources to digitizing their expansive collections with great focus on both audio and video documentary techniques, other organizations are following their lead when considering how the public may best access veterans' documented war experiences. Veterans oral history has also been included in curriculum databases. For example, the University of North Carolina at Chapel Hill's School of Education created *LEARNNC*, which was a program that included web resources that supports educators and communities to help improve K-12 education in North Carolina. Included is a digital textbook, *North Carolina History*, designed for eighth graders and beyond that covers all of North Carolina History. Five excerpts from my own oral history project were included in the digital textbooks under the theme "Postwar North Carolina/Vietnam War." These oral histories are supplemented with topics to consider as you read, questions to consider, as well as related topics. This digital textbook allows public access to these veterans oral histories while directly connecting their experiences to their home state. It has now been archived at *ANCHOR: A North Carolina History Online Resource*.

Veterans oral history also garners interest among the younger generation. Being media-oriented, this generation "seems to respond, absorb and be challenged more by visual images and sound than by the written word. As a result, the aurality of oral history will become increasingly important returning the 'voice' of the interviewees, narrators, and oral biographers to center stage." Given this return to aurality and the visual image, "technological breakthroughs point to re-centering of the narrator's voice. Veterans oral history offers an opportunity for more complex exploration of how people construct their narratives. 'Hearing' the silences and listening to intonation, pitch, and style of delivery adds an entirely new dimension to the sense we make of people's stories. This renewed focus places more emphasis on the recorded voices thus the creation on multiple oral history databases with public access to veterans' interviews" (Boyd and Larson).

Bibliography

Anchor: A North Carolina History Online Resource. www.ncpedia.org/anchor/vietnam-war. Accessed November 15, 2021.

Boyd, Douglas A, and Mary A. Larson, Eds. *Oral History and Digital Humanities: Voice, Access and Engagement*. New York, 2014.

Burnell, Karen J and Peter G. Coleman, and Nogel Hunt, "Coping with Traumatic Memories: Second World War Veterans' Experiences of Social Support in Relation to the

Narrative Coherence of War Memories." *Ageing & Society* vol. 30, no. 1, 2010, pp. 57–78. DOI: https://doi.org/10.1017/S0144686X0999016X

From Combat to Kentucky (C@Ky). www.uky.edu/veterans/content/c2k-combat-kentucky. Accessed by November 15, 2021.

McMillon, Harold. Personal interview. "Breaking the Silence: Unspoken Brotherhood of Vietnam Veterans." Oral History Project, Greenville, NC, 2002.

Oral History Association. www.oralhistory.org. Accessed November 7, 2021.

Ritchie, Donald. *Doing Oral History. A Practical Guide.* New York: Oxford UP, 2003.

Smith, Clark. "Oral History as 'Therapy': Combatants' Accounts of the Vietnam War." *Strangers at Home: Vietnam Veterans Since the War*, edited by Figley, Charles R., and Seymour Leventman. New York: Brunner/Mazel, 1990, pp. 17–19.

Tedeschi, R.G., and McNally, R.J., "Can We Facilitate Posttraumatic Growth in Combat Veterans?" *American Psychologist* vol. 66, no. 1, 2011, pp. 19–24.

The Veterans History Project at the Library of Congress. www.loc.gov/vets. Accessed November 07, 2021.

VOCES Oral History Project. https://voces.lib.utexas.edu. Accessed November 15, 2021.

Witness to War Foundation (WTW). www.witnesstowar.org. Accessed November 15, 2021.

Yvonne Latty, We Were There: *Voices of African Veterans, from World War II to the War in Iraq.* New York: HarperCollins, 2004.

15
REFLECTIONS

The Transformative Power of Veterans Oral History

There is a transformative power involved in oral history for veterans, interviewers, and listeners. For those who have already broken their silences, these narratives continue the legacy of truth. For those other veterans who have yet to come to terms with their war experiences, they can celebrate in the fact that others are speaking not only for them but also for all those soldiers who never returned home to speak for themselves. The stories are finally being told by the ones who experienced the war and not by those outside of the experience. During my oral history projects, veterans shared stories about their sense of isolation; returning home from a war zone without their unit; training in Parris Island (South Carolina) with a half dozen men who they did not want to get that close to; serving during the Tet Offensive and not wanting to know the names and faces of other men; how friendship across races did not survive the war; coming home during the Civil Rights Movement and being home on leave when Martin Luther King, Jr. was assassinated; having to do graves registration; being one of the first African Americans to join the reserves; being a young platoon sergeant trained in a medical company; bringing back everyone in their company whether they were wounded or not; writing in diaries allowed them to say, "I've come this far, I can survive another week;" not being told the truth about why they were fighting in Vietnam; listening to the Hanoi messages to convince them to stop fighting; how anger led to alcoholism, drugs, and isolation; having respect for the uniform; maybe exposing their wives and children to PTSD; and being young enough to kill but not old enough to legally buy alcohol. These veterans had faced their fears and spoken their experiences into existence.

The families and friends of war veterans also needed to hear these stories because, for some, these stories may be all they know or will ever know about their

DOI: 10.4324/9781003280323-19

loved ones who served. These stories are important because of the rapid decline in health of our war veterans, especially the older generations; exemplifies the need for veterans oral history; and can offer support, healing, and reconciliation about war experiences during storytelling sessions. With the loss of each war veteran comes the loss of undocumented and generational war experiences that contribute to our American military history.

Until the community forums were held during my oral history project, some families of veterans did not understand the depths of the wounds left by the war. The veterans shared some of their stories with those who were willing to listen. They shared their stories and for some families, and the veterans finally got the opportunity to hear why it was important for their stories to be told because their families needed healing, too. We heard a brother and sister, both in tears, talk about how they had never heard their father share any positive memories of Vietnam as some of the other veterans did. We learned that every soldier had his own war experiences and remembered them in personal ways. A woman talked about losing her husband, at the age of forty-eight, to complications due to exposure to Agent Orange. We heard several stories about veterans who felt rejected by the public and thus isolated themselves from their families for fear of further rejection. Some children of veterans came to hear things from other veterans that their own fathers would never tell them.

The forums gave the men and women a place not only to share stories but also to relinquish some of the burdens of war that they had carried for decades: the guilt of a squad leader at age of twenty-one witnessing the deaths of younger squad members; the responsibility of having another's life in one's hands; the courage to petition to go to Vietnam in place of a friend whose mother was ill in spite of racial strife he feared he might find; the shame that replaced the valor of war; the disappointment at never receiving a Purple Heart for which one had qualified; the utter confusion of being drafted at age nineteen and having to grow up instantly in the face of death; the chronic pains that are nightmarish reminders of war; the bravery of maintaining a silent code of honor to avoid further alienation; and the unpopularity back home about the war.

Children of veterans listened, learned, and cried as their parents embraced decades of despair right before their eyes. The community forums and storysharing session attracted veterans from other wars, too, who wanted to show their support. One veteran told me that after Vietnam he found it very difficult to form friendships with other men. The friendships that formed during the oral history project some thirty years after returning home from the war helped them not only with their current lives but it has also helped them look back on Vietnam with greater understanding.

Harold McMillon of the Greenville Veterans Outreach Center shared:

> The oral project works very closely with the Vet Centers. Their goal is to help the veteran and to let us know that we are not alone. We need to share our stories and experiences with our loved ones. I realize now that if we

reach out and not push away, just open up and not shut down and speak instead of being silent that we have family and friends who are waiting to accept us. It is a very slow process but it's working for me. Sharon feels that she now has family in many areas. She says to me that the veterans are her brothers, sisters, uncles and aunts and she is proud of them. I did not realize how much healing there is in getting together in groups or one-on-one to just talk to anyone that wants to be a part of what we have dealt with during war and at home. I now realize that all those years I spent fighting this battle alone only made me weaker and more angry. It sometimes takes a very strong man to admit that he needs help. I feel that all veterans should have the opportunity and privilege to sit down and share their memories with one another. I hope that there are more people that are willing to help and willing to keep on trying, even if we turn away from them at first, because it can be the turning point in a veteran's life for the better.

Vietnam Veteran Tex Howard (my uncle and Army retiree) once shared:

I was talking with my niece, Sharon, and she told me about the project, "Breaking the Silence: The Unspoken Brotherhood of Vietnam Veterans." My first thought was: Do I really want to get involved in this again? I didn't believe so, but after thinking about it for a while I decided to participate. I had not talked about my experiences in Vietnam for a very long time for several reasons. Mainly, I felt that the average person did not want to hear about Vietnam or wanted to hear about only the things that the veteran usually does not want to talk about. The impression I got when I returned home from the war was that we soldiers were a reminder of our country's mistakes in Vietnam, so if you get rid of the soldiers, you are no longer reminded of your mistakes. We ended up carrying the burdens of this country's mistakes. The soldiers suffered for something we did not create or ask for – we did not beg to go to Vietnam. We were sent there to do what we were asked to do, and now we continue to suffer for it. I've learned that veterans do not want to be reminded of bad things; we do not want to remember the hurtful things because it's like opening old wounds all over again. Thinking about it now, I could not figure out why I could barely remember certain things in an organized manner from my tours in Vietnam.

When I returned home in October 1968, I could have told about my experiences in an organized manner, but no one wanted to hear it. We will never completely get rid of it – we can never undo what happened all those years ago. The things that happened in Vietnam are cemented into our nervous systems and burned into our brains. We were thrown into war and then we were thrown back into society without any help in readjusting. The sad and pitiful thing about our experiences is that some of the men that survived Vietnam were not able to survive the aftershock of Vietnam. I must say none of this would have been possible if it had not been for my niece,

Louis's daughter, Sharon, who brought it all together. Now for the first time after 34 years, we're able to talk about Vietnam and not be ashamed. Thanks, Sharon, for not giving up on yourself and us. I have learned that maybe veterans need to seek help just to make life livable one day to the next. We need to learn how to deal with the past the best we can.

I cherished the stories the veterans told me because sharing them meant they trusted me. I have formed friendships with men and women who helped me better understand my father, and I feel as if I have gained brand new family members. I have always thought of myself as daddy's little girl, but since I started this work and projects, my father and I created a new relationship. He no longer just looked out for me; I was able to help him, too. We had so much more to talk about and my mother often joined the conversation. He was able to share more of himself with his family, and we had a lot of catching up to do. I never realized how much I did not know about my own father. My father once shared:

There are many reasons why Vietnam Veterans decided not to talk about our war experiences when we arrived home. For me, no one seemed to care about my time in Vietnam, especially people who hadn't themselves been vets. Everyone either looked at me like I had done something bad or they didn't believe what I had to say about my tour of duty. Usually people would ask questions like, "How many people did you kill?" I never would answer that question. People have mothers, fathers, brothers, and sisters, and I did not want to think about having taken that life from someone else, so I just kept quiet. I did not want Sharon to pursue her project at first. My daughter did not listen to me. Now the families of other veterans are grateful, and I am, too. But back then I knew that the veterans were not going to help her and that she would be rejected. I also knew that the rejection would hurt her, and I did not know how to protect her from that because I am good at rejecting people myself. I wanted to protect her from disappointment and hurt because I had already endured enough of that. Veterans did not talk to anyone except other veterans. We have felt too much rejection and hurt from our experiences. Too many stories are twisted the wrong way. We felt that no one cared for a veteran, especially a Vietnam Veteran, so it has become easy to reject anyone that did not understand us or listen to us about what we were feeling. Even though Sharon was rejected, she did not stop or give up. She had to gain the trust of the veterans and assure them that she was not only there to collect stories but to help others, including her own family. Once she earned their trust and confidence, she became a friend to the veterans. I am happy that someone is trying to understand the veterans and the reasons for their feelings about things. This project makes me and other veterans reach out and try to help each other understand that we are not alone. I will always be thankful to the staff at the Greenville and Raleigh Veterans Outreach Centers for supporting her.

These types of testimonies are what stayed with me throughout the years and continues to drive me to work with veterans. I was fortunate enough to have been able to spend time with wonderful human beings who have impacted my life in tremendous ways. After my father died, I often asked myself how do I get back to this work in order to finish it. He was no longer here to guide me through it, so it seemed quite difficult – if not impossible. Intellectually, I knew that my father and the other veterans might not live to see the end of this work but emotionally, I was hoping that they would. I have had to let my heart break into a million pieces just to breathe. However, I had to take those broken pieces and somehow figure out how to finish this book. I wanted to finish this book and return to working with veterans in a way that would best honor my father, but I was afraid that doing that might completely break me in a manner that I could not recover. With these feeling I often looked to my father for guidance and wondered what would he have to say about the importance of this work and why I should continue it. Since I have been doing this work, I think he would want me to continue to pass this knowledge along to others as he had done with me to teach others exactly what to when interviewing and talking to veterans about their wartime experiences. He would want me to focus on what others really need to know about their veteran when they are no longer here to tell their own stories. What happens when these veterans' voices are loss on a collective and grand, national scale? Who will continue to bear witness to their legacy of service after their death; who will be left to tell their stories? I allowed this to guide me in a way that, hopefully, has become not only my mourning song but also a manner by which others will be able to sense my loss and its profound significance, realizing that through veterans oral history my father's legacy continues to live.

Bibliography

Howard, Tex. Personal Interview. "Breaking the Silence: Unspoken Brotherhood of Vietnam Veterans." Oral History Project, Greenville, NC, 2002.

McMillon, Harold. Personal Interview. "Breaking the Silence: Unspoken Brotherhood of Vietnam Veterans." Oral History Project, Greenville, NC, 2002.

Raynor, Louis. Personal Interview. "Breaking the Silence: Unspoken Brotherhood of Vietnam Veterans." Oral History Project, Greenville, NC, 2002.

Appendices

APPENDIX A

Sample Interview Questionnaire

VETERANS ORAL HISTORY PROJECT

Biographical Details

1. What is your name?
2. Where/when were you born?
3. Who are you parents? What were their occupation?
4. What primary and secondary schools and/or college did you attend?
5. Did you have any jobs before entering service?

Early Days of Service

1. When did you join the military? Were you drafted or did you enlist?
2. What branch of the military did you serve?
3. If you enlisted, why did you join? Why did you select that branch to join?
4. What type of training or schooling did you receive?
5. What was your most vivid memory of your training or in school? What was the best part? What was the worst part?
6. What was your first assignment after basic training?
7. Did you receive any specialized training? If so, what?
8. Does any instructor or leader, during your training, stand out in your mind? If so, why?
9. Did you qualify with any equipment or weapons? If so, what was the training like?
10. What was the hardest part of your training?
11. Did you receive any promotions? Could you tell me more about that?
12. What was the hardest thing for you to adapt to when you first entered the service?

Wartime Service

1. When and where did you serve?
2. How many deployments or tours-of-duty did you complete?
3. Were you in a combat zone or support role?
4. Did you serve in a leadership capacity during your service/deployment?
5. Were you involved in any notable battles or conflicts during your service?
6. Is there a memorable incident that you would like to share? How did this incident change you?
7. Did you form any friendships during this time?
8. How did you stay in touch with your family and friends?
9. What did you do or where did you go during your off-duty or recreational time (R-n-R/or rest and recreation)?
10. Do you recall any particular humorous or unusual events?
11. What was the best part of your service experience?

After Service/Reflections

1. Do you recall the day your service ended? Where were you when your service ended?
2. Did you return home?
3. How were you received by your family and community?
4. How did you readjust to civilian life? Did you work or go back to school?
5. Did you G.I. Bill support your education?
6. How did your wartime experiences change you?
7. Did you continue any friendships from your time in service? Do you want to share a story about someone you stayed in touch with?
8. How did your service affect the way you related to or interacted with other people?
9. Did you join any veterans' organizations?
10. Did you attend any reunions?
11. How did your military service experiences affect your life?
12. What are some lessons you learned from your military service?
13. How has your military service impacted your feelings about war and military in general?
14. Is there anything that you want future generations to know about your military service?
15. Is there anything that you would like to add to your interview that we did not cover?
16. What would you like people to remember about your story?

Thank you for taking the time to share your recollections and military experiences.

APPENDIX B

Veteran's Biographical Information Form

VETERANS ORAL HISTORY PROJECT NAME	
NAME OF VETERAN	**CONTACT INFO (CURRENT RESIDENCE)**
OTHER NAMES KNOWN BY	**DATE/PLACE OF BIRTH**
BRANCH OF SERVICE	**YEARS IN SERVICE**
HIGHEST RANK	**UNIT, DIVISION, BATTALION, GROUP, SHIP, etc.**
COMMISSIONED ____ ENLISTED ____ DRAFTED____	**(Optional) RACE/ETHNICITY** **(Optional) GENDER**
TOURS OF DUTY/DEPLOYMENTS (WAR, OPERATION, CONFLICT)	
LOCATIONS OF MILITARY SERVICE	

RELEVANT BIOGRAPHICAL INFORMATION (AS IT RELATES TO THE GOALS OF THE PROJECT)
FAMILY/NEXT OF KIN (Full name, date of birth, relationship to interviewee)
EDUCATION (schools attended, degrees earned)
MEDALS OR SERVICE AWARDS
BATTLES/CAMPAIGNS
COMBAT or SERVICE-RELATED INJURIES SUSTAINED DURING WAR
SPECIAL DUTIES/ACHIEVEMENTS

Completed by:	Date:

APPENDIX C

Interviewer's Release Agreement Form

I, _____, an interviewer for
the_____ Veterans Oral History Project, understand and
agree to the following:

• I understand the goals and purposes of this project and understand I represent the
  oral history project when I am conducting an interview.
• I am willing to participate in a veterans oral history interviewer training.
• I understand the legal and ethical considerations regarding the interviews and will
  communicate them to and carry them out with each person I interview.
• I am willing to do the necessary preparation, including background research,
  for each interview I conduct.
• I will treat each interviewee with respect and I understand each interview will be
  conducted in a spirit of openness that will allow each interviewee to answer all
  questions as fully and freely as he or she wishes.
• I am aware of the need for confidentiality of interview content until such time as
  the interviews are released for public use (and/or any repository guidelines) and
  I will not exploit the interviewee's story.
• I understand my responsibilities regarding any archival materials or artifacts related
  to the interview that the interviewee may want to include in the interview process.
• I agree to submit all interview materials to the designated person and/or repository
  in a timely manner and to help facilitate all necessary processing and cataloging steps.

INTERVIEWER	ORAL HISTORY PROJECT
Name (print) _____	Name (print) _____
Signature _____	Signature _____
Date _____	Date _____

APPENDIX D

Veteran's Release Agreement Form

The mission of the _____(title of veterans oral history project) is to document the history of _____.
An important part of this effort is the collection of veterans oral history interviews with knowledgeable individuals.

    Thank you for participating in our project. Please read and sign this release form in order for your interview to be available for future use. Before doing so, you should read it carefully and ask any questions you may have regarding terms and conditions.

AGREEMENT

I, _____, interviewee, donate and convey my oral history interview dated, _____ to the _____
_____ (veterans oral history project/repository name). In making this gift I understand that I am conveying all right, title, and interest in copyright to the veterans oral history project/repository. I also grant the veterans oral history project/repository the right to use my name and likeness in promotional materials for outreach and educational materials. In return, the oral history project/repository grants me a non-exclusive license to use my interview through my lifetime.

    I further understand that I will have the opportunity to review and approve my interview before it is placed in the repository and made available to the public. Once approved, the veterans oral history project/repository will make my interview available for research without restriction. Future uses may include quotations in printed materials or audio/video excerpts in any media, and availability on the Internet.

(VETERAN) INTERVIEWEE	**INTERVIEWER**
Name (print) _____	Name (print) _____
Signature _____	Signature _____
Date _____	Date _____

APPENDIX E

Photograph and Memorabilia Log

VETERANS ORAL HISTORY PROJECT	
PROJECT NAME	
OWNER	
Name	
Address	Phone/Email
ITEM	
Type	Quantity
Detailed Description (Describe item and circumstances of loan)	
Associated Dates	
Physical Condition	
Instructions for use:	
RETURNED	
Items returned by (name):	
OWNER	INTERVIEWER
Name (print)	Name (print)
Signature	Signature
Date	Date

APPENDIX F

Interview Summary Form

VETERANS ORAL HISTORY PROJECT	
VETERANS ORAL HISTORY PROJECT NAME	
INTERVIEWEE (VETERAN)	**INTERVIEWER**
NAME (LIST OTHER NAMES KNOWN BY)	NAME
CONTACT INFO	CONTACT INFO
INTERVIEW DATE	INTERVIEW LENGTH
RECORDING MEDIUM Digital audio____ Digital video _____ Other_____	DELIVERY MEDIUM: Sound file _____Sound card _____ CD____DVD_____ Other_____
TECHNICAL NOTES (make/model of recorder, format recorded, microphone notes, etc.)	

INTERVIEW NOTES (physical environment/location, interruptions, veteran's mood, other people/animals in room)
DATE LEGAL RELEASE AGREEMENT SIGNED
PROPER NAMES AND KEYWORDS (personal and place names with proper spelling, dates, and keywords)
SUMMARY OF INTERVIEW CONTENT

Completed by:	Date:

APPENDIX G

Project Design Form

VETERANS HISTORY PROJECT
GENERAL
PROJECT NAME:
SPONSORING INSTITUTION:
PRIMARY GOAL:
MISSION STATEMENT:
ADMINISTRATIVE REQUIREMENTS:

PROJECT CONTENT
HISTORICAL FOCUS:
SCOPE:
TOPICS:
SOURCES FOR BACKGROUND RESEARCH:

PROJECT MANAGEMENT	
DURATION:	
NUMBER OF INTERVIEWEES:	
RECORDING PLAN:	
PHYSICAL SPACE NEEDS:	
EXPENSES:	
RESOURCES:	
INTERVIEWEE RECRUITMENT:	
REPOSITORY PLAN:	
ONLINE ACCESS FOR INTERVIEWS:	
Submitted by:	Date:
Received by:	Date:

APPENDIX H

Veterans Organization

National Call Center for Homeless Veterans.
www.va.gov/health/NewsFeatures/20120220a.asp
Disabled American Veterans (DAV)
www.dav.org
Black Veterans for Social Justice Inc.
www.bvsj.org
Iraq Veterans Against the War
www.ivaw.org
Japanese American Veterans Association (JAVA)
www.javadc.org/aboutus.htm
National Association for Black Veterans, Inc. (NABVETS)
www.nabvets.org
The Bunker Project
http://bunkerproject4vets.org/
The Society of Hispanic Veterans
www.hispanicveterans.org
Veterans for Peace
www.veteransforpeace.org
Veterans for Commonsense
http://veteransforcommonsense.org
Women Veterans of America
www.womenveteransofamerica.com
National Center for PTSD
www.ptsd.va.gov
Soldier's Heart
www.soldiersheart.net

United Children of Veterans
www.unitedchildrenofveterans.com
Veterans' Children
www.veteranschildren.com
Veterans Crisis Line
1-800-273-8355
www.veteranscrisisline.net

APPENDIX I

Oral History Organizations

Oral History Association www.oralhistory.org
Canadian Oral History Association (United States)
www.oralhistorycentre.ca/oral_history_forum_project
International Oral History Association www.ioha.org
Oral History in the Mid-Atlantic Region (OHMAR) https://ohmar.org
Oral History Society (Great Britain) www.ohs.org.uk
Oral History Association of Australia www.oralhistoryaustralia.org.au
Southwest Oral History Association www.southwestoralhistory.org
Center for Oral History, University of Connecticut www.oralhistory.uconn.edu
Oral History Index www.vcmha.org/oralhist.html
American Communities: An Oral History www.duke.edu/web/hstl95.15/
Behind the Veil-Home Page http://www-cds.aas.duke.edu/btv/
Center for Oral History, University of Connecticut www.oralhistory.uconn.edu
Baylor University Institute for Oral History www.baylor.edu/oralhistory/
American Society for State and Local History http://about.aaslh.org
American Historical Society www.historians.org
The History Channel www.history.com
American Folklore Society www.afsnet.org
Oral History in the Digital Age http://ohda.matrix.msu.edu

SELECTED BIBLIOGRAPHY

Aberbach, David. *Surviving Trauma: Loss, Literature, and Psychoanalysis*. New Haven: Yale UP, 1989.

Allison, Fred H. "We Listen to What Marines Say: The Marine Corps Oral History Program." *Marine Corps Gazette* vol. 89 no. 6, 2005, pp. 4–55.

Altschuler, Glenn S., and Stuart M. Blumin. *The GI Bill: A New Deal for Veterans*. New York: Oxford University Press, 2009.

Anderson, Kathryn and Dana Jack. "Learning to Listen: Interview Techniques and Analyses." In *The Oral History Reader*, edited by Robert Parks and Alistair Thomson. New York: Routledge, 1998, pp. 157–171.

Barone, Thomas. "Persuasive Writings, Vigilant Readings, and Reconstructed Characters: The Paradox of Trust in Educational Storysharing." In *Life History and Narrative*, edited by J. Amos Hatch and Richard Wisniewski. London: The Falmer Press, 1995, pp. 63–74.

Bennett, James. "Human Values in Oral History." *The Oral History Review* vol. 11, 1983, pp. 1-15.

Bergen, Teresa. *Transcribing Oral History*. New York: Routledge, 2020.

Bragin, Martha. "Can Anyone Here Know Who I Am? Co-constructing Meaningful Narratives with Combat Veterans." *Clinical Social Work Journal* vol. 38, 2010, pp. 316–326.

Brende, Joel Osler, and Erwin Randolph Parson. *Vietnam Veterans: The Road to Recovery*. New York: Plenum Press, 1985.

Brinker, William J. "Oral History and the Vietnam War." *Magazine of History* vol. 11, no. 3, 1997, pp. 15–19.

Burnell, Karen J., Peter G. Coleman and Nigel Hunt. "Coping with Traumatic Memories: Second World War Veterans' Experiences of Social Support in Relation to the Narrative Coherence of War Memories." *Ageing and Society* vol. 30, no. 1, 2010, pp. 57–78.

Caruth, Cathy. *Unclaimed Experience: Trauma, Narrative, and History*. Baltimore, MD: Johns Hopkins UP, 1996.

Coffman, Edward M. "Talking about War: Reflections on Doing Oral History and Military History." *The Journal of American History* vol. 87, no. 2, 2000, pp. 582–592.

Davis, Roger, Mark R. Ellis, and Linda van Ingen. "Civic Engagement and Task Force Teaching: Integrating the Veterans History Project into the University Classroom." *The History Teacher* vol. 42, no. 3, 2009, pp. 341–349.

Dunaay, David K., and Willa K. Baum, eds., *Oral History: An Interdisciplinary Anthology*. Walnut Creek, CA: AltaMira Press, 1996.

Egendorf, Arthur. *Healing From the War: Trauma and Transformation After Vietnam*. Boston, MA: Houghton Mifflin, 1985.

Erikson, Kai. *Everything in Its Path: Destruction of Community in the Buffalo Creek Flood*. New York, NY: Simon & Schuster, 1978.

Estes, Steve. "Ask and Tell: Gay Veterans, Identity, and Oral History on a Civil Rights Frontier." *Oral History Review* vol. 32, no. 2, 2005, pp. 21–47.

Fish, Lydia. "The Vietnam Veterans Oral History Project and Folklore Project." *Voices* vol. 30, no. 3 and 4, 2004, pp. 6–7.

Gilmore, Leigh. *The Limits of Autobiography: Trauma and Testimony*. Ithaca, NY: Cornell UP, 2001.

Gluck, Sherna Berger, Donald A. Ritchie, and Bret Eynon. "Reflections on Oral History in the New Millennium: Roundtable Comments." *The Oral History Review* vol. 26, no. 2, 1999, pp. 1–27.

Grimsley, Reagan L. and Wynne, Susan C. "Creating Access to Oral Histories in Academic Libraries." *College & Undergraduate Libraries* vol. 16, no. 4, 2009, pp. 278–99.

Hagopian, Patrick. "Oral Narratives: Secondary Revision and the Memory of the Vietnam War." *History Workshop* vol. 32, 1991, pp. 134–150.

Hagopian, Patrick. "Voices from Vietnam: Veterans' Oral Histories in the Classroom." *The Journal of American History* vol. 87, no. 2, 2000, pp. 593–601.

Herman, Judith, *Trauma and Recovery: The Aftermath of Violence-from Domestic to Political Terror*. New York: Basic Books, 1997.

Hitchcock, Peter. *Dialogics of the Oppressed*. Minneapolis: U of Minnesota P, 1993.

Houston, Marsha, and Cheris Kramarae. "Speaking From Silence: Methods of Silencing and of Resistance." *Discourse & Society* vol. 2, no. 4, 1991, pp. 387–399.

Hunt, Nigel, and Ian Robbins. "Telling stories of the War: Ageing Veterans Coping With Their Memories Through Narrative." *Oral History* vol. 26, no. 2, 1998, pp. 57–64.

Hynes, Samuel. "Personal Narratives and Commemoration." In *War and Remembrance in the Twentieth Century*, edited by Jay Winter and Emmanuel Sivan. Cambridge: Cambridge UP, 1999, pp. 205–220.

Kuenning, Delores A. *Life After War: How Veterans and Their Loved Ones Can Heal the Psychological Wounds of War*. New York: Paragon House, 1991.

Kuhn, Clifford. "Let's Get Digital! Possibilities and Problems of Oral History in the Digital Age." *Provenance: Journal of the Society of Georgia Archivists* vol. 31, no. 2, 2013, pp. 96–108.

Kuzmaraov, Jeremy. *The Myth of the Addicted Army: Vietnam and the Modern War on Drugs*. Amherst: University of Massachusetts Press, 2009.

Laub, Dori. "Bearing Witness or the Vicissitudes of Listening." In *Testimony: Crisis of Witnessing in Literature, Psychoanalysis, and History*, edited by Shoshana Felman, and Dori Laub. New York: Routledge, 1992, pp. 57–74.

Laub, Dori. "Truth and Testimony: The Process and the Struggle." In *Trauma: Explorations in Memory*, edited by Cathy Caruth. Baltimore, MD: Johns Hopkins UP, 1995, pp. 61–75.

Lembcke, Jerry. *The Spitting Image: Myth, Memory, and the Legacy of Vietnam*. New York: New York University Press, 1998.

Lorde, Audre. "The Transformation of Silence Into Language and Action." In *Sister Outsider: Essays and Speeches*, edited by Audre Lorde. Freedom, CA: The Crossing Press, 1984, pp. 40–44.

Lynch, Michael. "Every Soldier Has a Story: Creating a Veterans History Project." *Magazine of History* vol. 22, no. 4, 2008, p. 37.

MacKay, Nancy, Barbara W. Sommer, and Mary Kay Quinlan. *Community Oral History Toolkit*. London: Routledge, 2013.

MacKay, Nancy. *Curating Oral Histories: From Interview to Archive*. 2nd ed. London: Routledge, 2016.

Matasaki, Aphrodite. *Vietnam Wives: Women and Children Surviving Life With Veterans Suffering Post-Traumatic Stress Disorder*. Bethesda, MD: Woodbine House, 1988.

Musheno, Michael and Susan Ross. *Deployed: How Reservists Bear the Burden of Iraq: Shadows of Vietnam*. Ann Arbor: University of Michigan Press, 2009.

Nespor, Jan and Liz Barber. "Audience and the Politics of Narrative." In *Life History and Narrative*, edited by J. Amos Hatch and Richard Wisniewsk. London: The Falmer Press, 1995, pp. 49–62.

Neuenschwander, John A. *A Guide to Oral History and the Law*. 2nd ed. Oxford: Oxford University Press, 2014.

Nicosia, Gerald. *Home to War: A History of the Vietnam Veterans Movement*. New York: Crown, 2001.

Parker, Christopher S. *Fighting for Democracy: Black Veterans and the Struggle Against White Supremacy*. Princeton, NJ: Princeton University Press, 2009.

Parr, Allison. "Breaking the Silence: Traumatised War Veterans and Oral History." *Oral History (War and Masculinities)* vol. 35, no. 1, 2007, pp. 61–70.

Rice, Gary. "War, Journalism, and Oral History." *The Journal of American History* vol. 87, no. 2, 2000, pp. 610–613.

Ritchie, Donald. *Doing Oral History*. 3rd ed. London: Oxford UP, 2014.

Samuel, Raphael. "Local History and Oral History." *History Workshop* vol. 1, no. 976, pp. 191-208.

Schram, Martin. *Vets Under Siege: How America Deceives and Dishonors Those Who Fight Our Battles*. New York: St. Martin's Press, 2008.

Shopes, Linda. "After the Interview Ends Moving Oral History Out of the Archives and Into Publication." *The Oral History Review* vol. 42, no. 2, 2015, pp. 300–310.

Smith, Clark. "Oral History as 'Therapy': Combatants' Accounts of the Vietnam War." In *Strangers at Home: Vietnam Veterans since the War*, edited by Figley, Charles R. and Seymour Leventman. New York: Brunner/Mazel, 1990, pp. 9–34.

Sommer, Barbara W. *Doing Veterans Oral History*. Bangalore: Oral History Association, 2015.

Sommer, Barbara W. *Practicing Oral History in Historical Organizations*. New York: Routledge, 2015.

Sommer, Barbara W. and Mary Kay Quinlan. *The Oral History Manual*. Lanham: Rowman & Littlefield, 2018.

Stein, Alan H. and Gene B. Pruess. "Race, Poverty and Oral History." *Poverty & Race Research Action Council* vol. 15, no. 5, 2006, pp. 1–11.

Summerskill, Clare. *Creating Verbatim Theatre From Oral Histories*. New York: Routledge, 2020.

Tal, Kali. *Worlds of Hurt: Reading the Literatures of Trauma*. Cambridge: Cambridge UP, 1996.

Tedeschi, Richard. "Posttraumatic Growth in Combat Veterans." *Journal of Clinical Psychology Medical Setting* vol. 18, 2011, pp. 137–144.

Tedeschi, Richard G. and Richard J. McNally. "Can We Facilitate Posttraumatic Growth in Combat Veterans?" *American Psychologist* vol. 66, no. 1, 2011, pp. 19–24.

Thompson, Paul. "The Voice of the Past: Oral History." In *The Oral History Reader*, edited by Robert Parks, and Alistair Thomson. New York: Routledge, 1998, pp. 21–28.

Turner, Fred. *Echoes of Combat: Trauma, Memory, and the Vietnam War*. Minneapolis, MN: U of Minnesota P, 1996.

v. 1. *Introduction to Community Oral History*.

v. 2. *Planning a Community Oral History Project*.

v.3. *Managing a Community Oral History Project.*

v.4. *Interviewing in Community Oral History.*

v.5. *After the Interview in Community Oral History.*

Whitfield, Toni S. and Annick D. Conis. "War Veterans' Memoirs as Narrated to Students: An Intergenerational Service-Learning Project for Interpersonal Communication." *Communication Teacher* vol. 20, no. 1, 2006, pp. 23–27.

Wilson, Robert M. "The Veterans Education Project of Amherst, Massachusetts." *Historical Journal of Massachusetts* vol. 41, no. 2, 2013, pp. 73–82.

Winter, Jay and Emmanuel Sivan, "Setting the Framework." In *War and Remembrance in the Twentieth Century*, edited by Jay Winter and Emmanuel Sivan. Cambridge: Cambridge UP, 1999, pp. 6–39.

Young, Sandra. "Writing Lives of Others: The Veterans Project." *Pedagogy* vol. 3, no. 1, 2003, pp. 73–84.

Zieren, Gregory R. "Negotiating Between Generations: A Decade of Experience Teaching Oral History." *Oral History Review* vol. 38, no. 1, 2011, pp. 158–174.

INDEX

Made in the USA
Middletown, DE
05 October 2023

40240551R00102